MW01643785

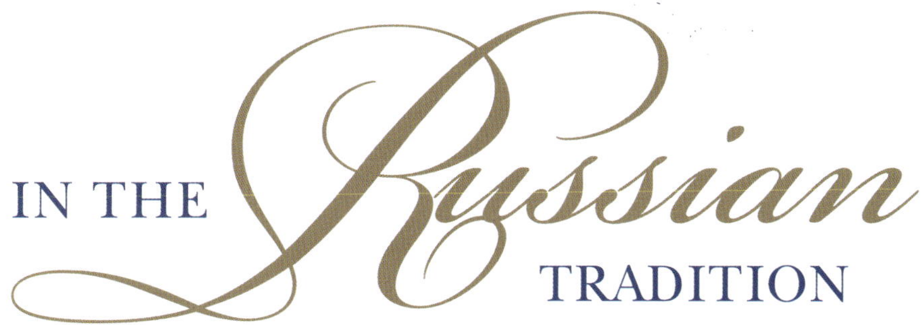

A Historic Collection
of 20th Century
Russian Painting

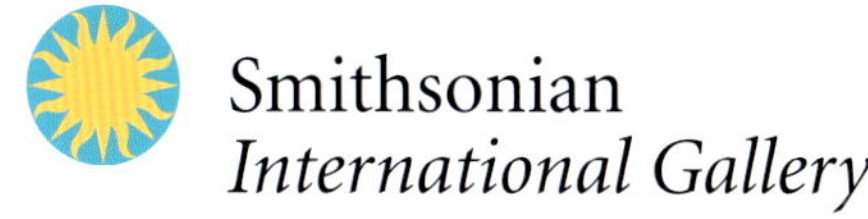

Washington, D.C.
December 15, 2004 - March 20, 2005

Exhibition Concept — Aleksandr Morozov, Maria Bulanova

Director General, The State Tretyakov Gallery — Valentin Rodionov

President, The Russian Museum of Art — Bradford Shinkle IV

Academic Supervisor, The State Tretyakov Gallery — Aleksandr Morozov

Letters of Greeting
The State Tretyakov Gallery — Valentin Rodionov
The Museum of Russian Art — Raymond E. Johnson
The International Gallery, Smithsonian Institution — Ellen Nixon Dorn

Exhibition Curators — Natalia Aleksandrova, Maria Bulanova

Academic Editor — Dr. Aleksandr Morozov

Essays — John Bowlt, Maria Bulanova, Mikhail German, Aleksandr Morozov

Catalogue text — Natalia Aleksandrova, Maria Bulanova

Catalog Design — Dmitry Melnik, Bill Moeger

Exhibition Coordination — Maria Bulanova, Tatiana Gubanova, Nikolai Bulanov participating

Editor and Publishing Supervisor — Joan Lee

Technical Supervisor — Reed Fellner

Translator and Production Supervisor — Nikolai Bulanov, "Pro-text"

We are deeply grateful for the support of our participating sponsors.

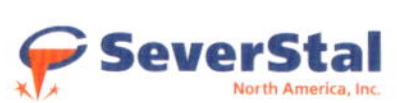

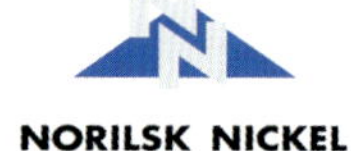

NORILSK NICKEL

We sincerely appreciate the extraordinary efforts of the following for their contributions to this exhibition:

From the Russian Embassy:
Ambassador Yuri Ushakov, Senior Counselor Boris Marchuk and First Secretary, Culural Attache Irina Popova.

From the Smithsonian Institution:
Ellen Nixon Dorn, Betsy Burstein Robinson, Seth Waite, Linda St. Thomas, Nell Payne, Mary Bird, Bonnie Kelso, Roslynn Correa, Stephen Wood, Angela Roberts and Amy Ballard.

From The State Tretyakov Gallery:
Galina Andreeva, Galina Churak, Tatiana Gubanova, Irina Lebedeva, Ekaterina Selezneva and Natalia Soukhova.

From The Museum of Russian Art:
Douglas Johnson, Scott Nagel, Reed Fellner, Ginny Tyson, Jane Frees-Kluth, Joline Neve Terry Benson and Peter Schmidt.

ISBN 0-9721493-1-7

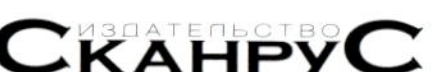

Printed in Korea

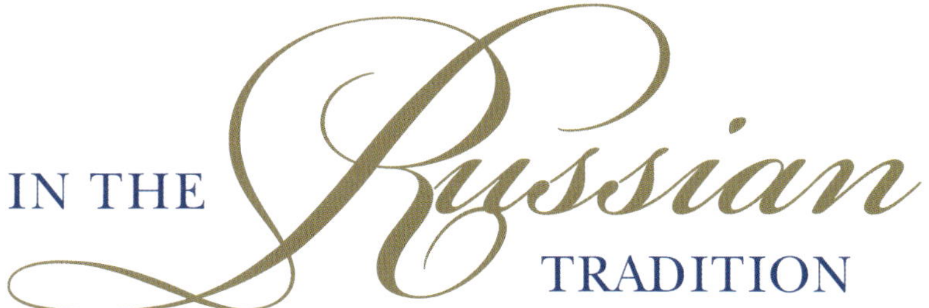

A Historic Collection
of 20th Century
Russian Painting

Contents

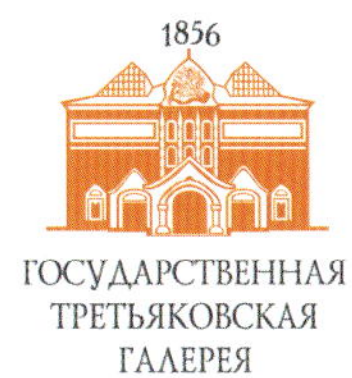

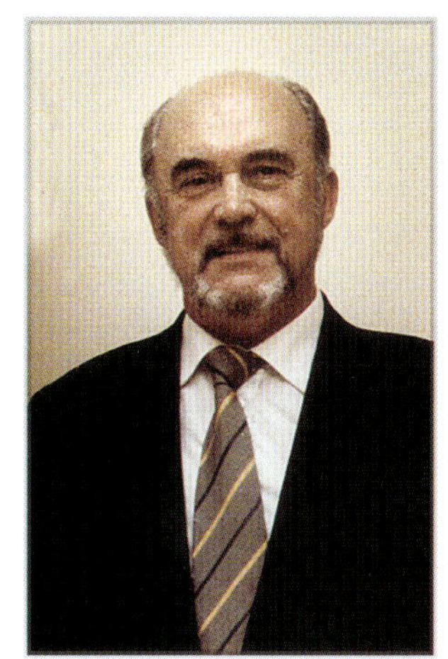

The exhibition, "In The Russian Tradition: A Historic Collection of 20th Century Russian Paintings" is devoted to paintings by the outstanding Russian artists of the period. The State Tretyakov Gallery, the museum that holds the national collection of Russian art masterpieces, is pleased to present to the American public the art of generations of painters from the late 19th century to the 1970s. Paintings by Ilya Repin, Valentin Serov, Kuzma Petrov-Vodkin, and Filipp Malyavin demonstrate the highest level of mastery. They became as a truly national phenomenon, the source of the traditional and, at the same time, innovative paintings of Aleksandr Deineka, Aristarkh Lentulov and others who worked in the 1930s and 1940s.

In the 1950s and 1960s the national tradition and avant garde innovative pictorial devices were associated with artistic freedom and weakened the officially dictated ideologies. To a great extent these devices shaped Russian art of the late 20th century.

We would like to draw your attention to Russian artists' reflections regarding how people managed to preserve their humanity on the tragic paths of 20th century Russian history. The exhibition should demonstrate to the American viewers that many of the important developments in 20th century Russian art had nothing to do with political issues of the period. Russian art is an integral part of the world artistic context, the fundamentals of which always have been human life, the world that surrounds us, life and death.

We are pleased to partner with The Museum of Russian Art (Minneapolis) which is providing 23 paintings by some of the greatest artists of the second half of the 20th century, such as Geli Korzhev, Vasili Nechitailo, Sergei and Aleksei P. Tkachev, and Vladimir Stozharov. We are honored by the serious interest this museum has taken in this period, and we are especially grateful for the generosity of Raymond E. Johnson in lending portions of his collection to our museum.

We also express our appreciation specifically to Mr. Johnson for his support of The State Tretyakov Gallery in his efforts to raise funds for the restoration of the Grozny Museum of Art in Chechnya, which sustained damages from military action during the war.

Also on behalf of The Tretyakov Gallery I would like to thank our colleagues from the Smithsonian Institution for their interest and support of this exhibition. We are most grateful to the embassy of the Russian Federation in Washington, D.C. and especially to Ambassador Extraordinary and Plenipotentiary Mr. U.V. Ushakov and Senior Counselor B.U. Marchuk for all their assistance.

Valentin Rodionov

Director General, The State Tretyakov Gallery
Member of the Russian Academy of Arts

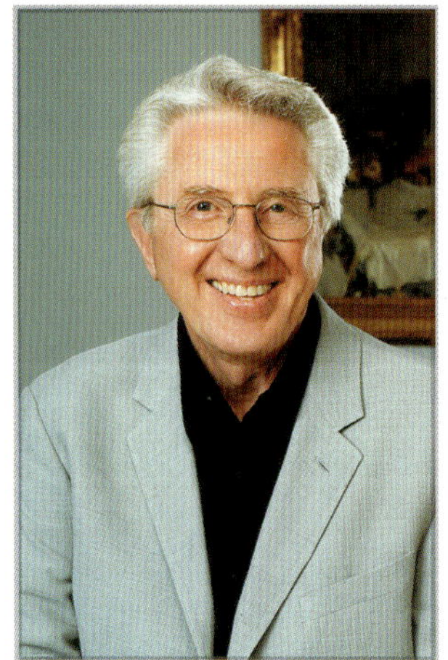

The Museum of Russian Art

My wife, Susan, and I have long admired the contributions of Russian writers, musicians and dancers that have justifiably earned a reputation for excellence among a wide cross section of international critics. Our personal interest in Russian 19th century and avant-garde painting peaked during the 1980's when we became curious about the relative absence of English language scholarship regarding 20th century Russian realist art.

In 1991 we acquired a modest number of Russian Impressionist paintings that subsequently became the core of our personal art collection. What started as a historical inquiry into international art development has become one of the compelling interests in our lives. The Johnson Collection has evolved into a unique compendium of the Russian creative genius including artistic examples from more than 100 years of the Russian painting tradition.

As individual collectors, Susan and I have experienced the continuing pleasure of discovering and appreciating the technical brilliance and historical significance of Russian paintings. We have derived an equal degree of fulfillment to the extent that we have been able to share our enthusiasm for these paintings with the American public. In 2002 we founded The Museum of Russian Art to become the institutional host for our collection. The museum maintains continuous exhibitions of Russian art and artifacts in an effort to present Americans with an expanded opportunity to see and learn about significant elements of Russian society and history. These paintings capture a perspective of Russia that is frequently different from the traditional view of that country held by Americans. My hope is that our exhibitions serve to increase the appreciation by both Russian and American citizens of the universality of our shared human emotions and experiences.

Our museum events have also created opportunities for exciting collaborations with representatives of the international museum community. We are pleased that we have been able to assist The State Tretyakov Gallery in presenting this exhibition, "In the Russian Tradition"

Please accept my invitation to visit The Museum of Russian Art whenever you are in the Minneapolis area.

Sincerely,

Raymond E. Johnson

Raymond E. Johnson
Founder

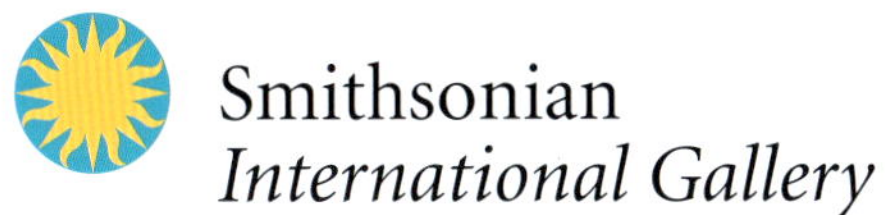

Over the past twelve years, my office has coordinated and presented an average of fifteen exhibitions a year here at the Smithsonian Institution. These exhibitions have run the gamut of themes–science, art, history, culture, and more. Few have inspired me the way this exhibition, "In the Russian Tradition: A Historic Collection of 20th Century Russian Paintings" does. The more I discover, the more excited I get. The works in this exhibition are colorful and lively, expressing a world about which I want to learn more.

My hope is that this exhibition will educate many more people and open up a whole new world for them. I trust that it will not only spark their interest in Russian art, but that it will lure them into the process of learning more about the Russian culture in general. All it takes is a spark!

The Smithsonian Institution is proud to present this beautiful and important exhibition here in our International Gallery. Hopefully, those who experience the exhibition will be encouraged to visit The Museum of Russian Art in Minneapolis, and if they are really lucky, to visit The State Tretyakov Gallery in Moscow. Enjoy the exhibition.

Sincerely,

Ellen Nixon Dorn
Director of the International Gallery

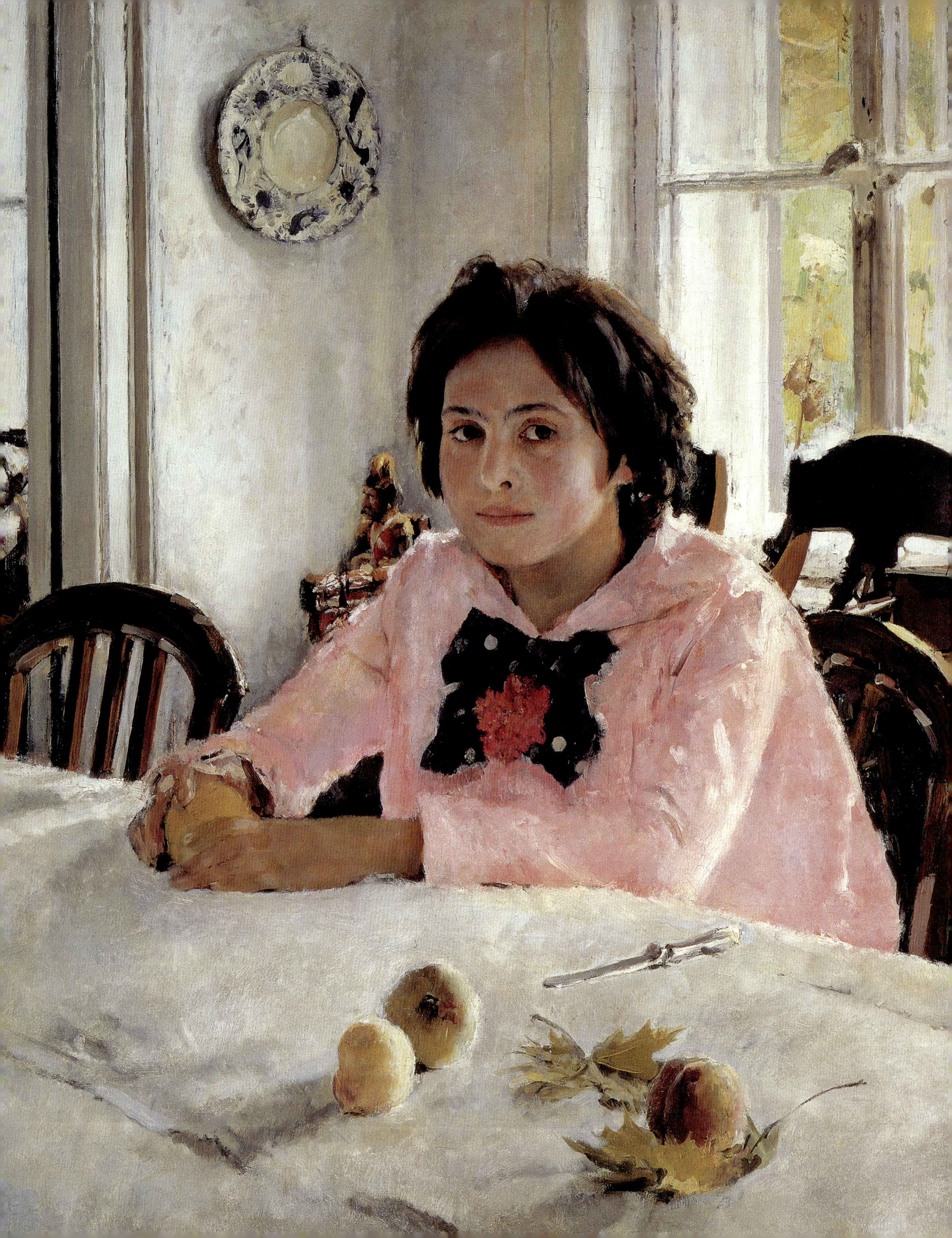

The Traditions of 20th Century Russian Art

Aleksandr Morozov

A shift in subject matter in the 1880s was occasioned by Russian artists' shift in genre preferences. Before this time, an artist would prefer to contemplate the natural world and acknowledge his lyrical creed through landscape images. But in the 1880s, artists' efforts turned to the subject of human personality. The most significant artists of the time concentrated on what can be called "a philosophical portrait" and "the choir," multi-figure compositions with important social and historical content. "Choir" was the term applied by Vladimir Stasov, one of the period's leading art critics and an ideological leader of the Wanderers.

It should be mentioned here that only a few masters of the time, who held lofty ideological positions, were forced to be pedant teachers of life. Most artists were predisposed to an open and lively realism that depicted passion for life in all kinds of subjects. The most important feature of Ilya Repin's unique gift for portraiture was his open-minded approach to every authentic personality's manifestations, observing and capturing all qualities of talent and beauty. Two of Repin's paintings in this exhibition demonstrate his mastery of the fundamentals of the Russian painting tradition: his portraits of the charming French pianist and the young Vladimir Stasov, who championed his "truth."

It should also be mentioned that Russian realism, as a reproduction of visual reality, is mutable, with subject matter historically determined by the personal preferences of the artists themselves. About the mid-19th century, Russian realism depended to a certain extent on the formal and old-fashioned language of the academic school. But as early as the 1870s, Russian genres and landscape painters were becoming more enchanted with the "enlightened" art of the Barbizon school, and the exotically bold (for those times) compositional and color discoveries of Eduard Manet. Later, for a number of reasons, a passion for French Impressionism would remain critical to Russian painting, especially in the USSR where, by the way, it wasn't officially encouraged at all. A viewer might note in Mika Morozov's portrait, a masterpiece by Repin's best student, Serov, a certain symbiosis of impressionistic freshness with the best characteristics of Russian realism. But on the other hand, one of the most enduring examples of impressionism introduced in Russia is *Snow in March* by Igor Grabar, painted in the early 1900s.

To summarize, we would venture to say that for many Russian artists this dogma has remained sacred, when compared to the fulfillment of their most courageous and fascinating aspirations. And vice versa: the genius of such intentions marking the revolutionary peaks of artistic avant-garde is discovered if we manage to understand the existential and philosophical ideas that prompted them. Take, for example, *Black Square* by Malevich and *Tower of the Third International* by Tatlin. It should also be pointed out that it was not only in the early period, but also in their later years that both great innovators refer to the figurative and pictorial style that is usually called realism. Such a "regressive" turn late in their lives was, for themselves, controversial and deeply dramatic. Still, this doesn't prevent many serious researchers from venerating Malevich's "peasant

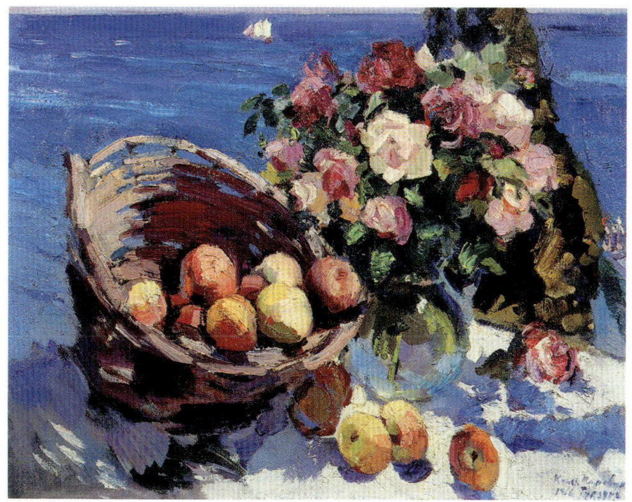

Valentin SEROV. **Girl with Peaches.** 1887. Detail
Oil on canvas. 35½ x 33⅛ in. (91 x 85 cm)

Konstantin KOROVIN. **Gurzuf.** 1916
Oil on canvas. 26⅛ x 34⅜ in. (67 x 88 cm)

series" painted in the late 1920s and early 1930s, as well as Tatlin's art of the 1930s and 1940s. In addition, Chagall, both in his Russian and foreign periods, never broke with his figurative style, as did Pavel Filonov, who stayed in Russia until the end of his life. His *Gates of Narva, Faces* and *Kolkhoznik* are held up as examples of 20th century realism. However, it was not considered "socialist realism" in the USSR.

There is enough evidence to say that in the 20th century, as well as in the 19th, the figurative, pictorial and realistic styles, although they may vary, have remained basic to fine art in Russia, the USSR, and then Russia again. It is this style that differentiates the Russian artistic tradition from those seen in other cultures. This does not negate or lessen the importance of other artistic styles. There were many, and they left monuments worthy of great interest. But here a certain fundamental is discussed that gave power, especially in the most dramatic moments in history, to the Russian pictorial tradition.

The period from the late 19th century to the early years of the 20th century was a time of tectonic shifts in Russian art. After the stimulus of impressionism, the refreshing elements were Cezanne's post-impressionism, early cubism, modern style; symbolism in its Scandinavian, Belgium and German variants; and its own emerging expressionism. Filipp Malyavin is of great interest at this stage, and the interest is based on his manner of painting and even a certain exotic quality in his art. The artist neither stayed away from the popularity of Anders Zorn, nor from the decorative element of modernism that served as a pattern to create his own variation of heterogeneous, flat paintings, nor Russian primitive art, where his characters' faces and the bright colors in many of his paintings originate. But at the same time, his "girls" are very Russian paintings. They contain a broad hint of Raseya (Russia) by Boris Grioriev. They introduce the cold element of *Green Noise* by Nekrasov into the hot flame of Malyavin's own *Round Dance*, as if it should somehow correspond to Rachmaninoff's "Spring" cantata that was written at almost the same time.

One of the masterpieces of the exhibition, *The Bathing of the Red Horse*, by Petrov-Vodkin, also originates from the historical period in which it was created. The painting is difficult to interpret, although as early as 1912, when it was finished, it was believed to be one of the most important and best painted of new Russian works. The artist himself explained it many times, each time in a different way, though he seems to have said nothing understandable. *The Bathing of the Red Horse* is driven away from realism by a powerful symbolic and decorative element: a red horse representing a version of a well-known iconic motif, St. George the Victor. This theme also puts the painting into the context of Russian religious and national art that Petrov-Vodkin greatly appreciated. Still, the red horse itself hardly removes the realistic element; the modernist and iconic, and decorative, solid monolithic character of the picture casts a spell on the viewer. Undoubtedly, it was an achievement by the artist, who knew of Matisse's passion for Russian icons and saw the latest French paintings both at home and abroad, in the first Jack of Diamonds exhibitions and also in recognized private collections. The painting appeared as it was made in Russia, but hardly worse than if it has been painted in France. But the composition and color of *The Bathing of the Red Horse* draw a veil over the mystery: the horse appears powerful, romantic and beautiful. But what abut the nude boy riding it?

Probably it is here that the artist offers the principal contrast hardly understood by both today's public and his own contemporaries. Vodkin's young character and the horse come from two completely different worlds. The critics at the time paid little attention to the type of the portrait. The language of the painting, in general, is affirmatively monumental. But the portrait itself seems to be taken somewhere from another exhibition. And it doesn't take long to find it. It was in one of the World of Art shows. The critics have nearly forgotten that Petrov-Vodkin chose one of his pupils, S. Kalmykov, as a model. The boy looks very much like young St. Petersburg bohemians who are often seen on canvases and works on paper by K. Somov, M. Dobuzhinsky, B. Kustodiev, etc.

This is how, inside Petrov-Vodkin, a realist was born (intentionally or by chance), and it makes for a reinterpretation of this famous painting that leads to a simple explanation. For nearly half a century this painting was not exhibited because of its "formalism," that ever-ambiguous term that hints of something iconic or modernist. At last, when the public managed to see the painting at the end of Khrushchev era (thanks to the brilliant art critic and historian Vladimir Kostin) they started to interpret it as a symbol of future revolutionary fires. But it would be far more correct to compare him to the polyphonic, but fragile, harmonies by Skryabin, complicated by tragic implications. The composer wrote one of his most philosophical scores, *A Poem of Fire*, in 1910, almost at the same time.

Still the ideological difficulties and closely related temptations of political engagement that sooner or later constrain every form and style of art appear to have accompanied Russian realism from its very birth. As for the artists, to survive as one they didn't turn to some alternative dissident ideas, but instead they tried to remove ideology from their art, tried to dive into the themes of life that were a kind of escape to nature. This can be seen as yet another "Russian tradition," especially in the Soviet 20th century. This specific drama of the "revolutionary" Russian culture was evident to Prince S. Volkonski, a noted man of the theatre in the early 20th century. In the 1920s, he wrote in his journal: "What can be more beautiful than nature nowadays, what can be more relaxing than its indifference to party memberships."

Obviously, in different periods of time such oppositions show themselves in various forms, and our exhibition proves it well. The way an artistic evolution was to develop had depended on many things. First, time itself made certain transformations in the general atmosphere of ideas and moods within society and that shaped basic artistic vectors. Thus we are able to understand why there were futuristic and constructivist tendencies in the 1920s, a shift to a more classical orientation in the early 1950s and artistic turmoil in the 1960s and 1970s. The last period seems to have filled the notable gaps of the historical and latest artistic experience in the Russian-Soviet artists' collective mentality. Secondly, the formal qualities of the realistic vision itself evolved because living artists' mentalities searched for new ways to reproduce reality. Of course, with every new generation the "truthful vision" changed.

What happened in Russian and Soviet art depended greatly on society's political history. I mean both global shake-ups in world history of the 20th century as well as their interaction with the pulsating history of the Bolshevik state. The state always influenced objective cultural developments. At the same time, here a sincere belief in social progress and the manipulations of propaganda often mixed, prompting a struggle between various social forces. Usually it wasn't absolutely clear which one actually was victorious. Accordingly, the history of Soviet art appears to be rather entangled, and many of its periods and stages didn't coincide with global cultural developments. What "suddenly" became urgent in Soviet art of the mid- and late 20th century had actually been born decades earlier, but didn't continue "from youth to old age," thus sometimes resulting in paradoxical artistic situations. The great Shostakovich is reported to have said: "One should live in Russia for a long time." This is reasonable: in this country people should have to wait for finality for a long time. This even more impedes understanding of the complicated developments in Russian-Soviet culture as compared to "classical" Western models where artistic movements changed gradually. The image of Western artistic development was determined by museums of modern art worldwide a long time ago.

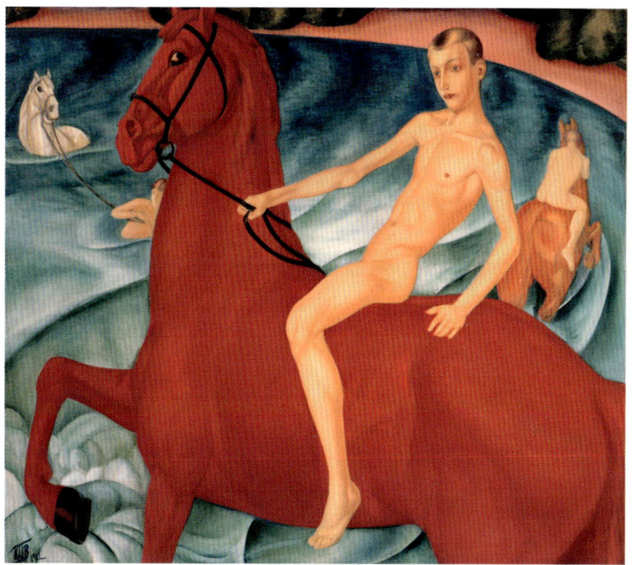

Kuzma PETROV-VODKIN. **The Bathing of the Red Horse**. 1912
Oil on canvas. 62½ x 72½ IN. (160 x 186 cm)

An interesting mass of contradictions is presented by a group of paintings whose artists all belonged to the "neo-primitivism" movement of the 1910s and were somehow related to the Jack of Diamonds group that included M. Larionov, A. Lentulov, V. Rozhdestvenski, R. Falk and P. Konchalovski. Early works of the first two demonstrate a parody and play on the origins of the "Jacks." At the same time, Lentulov focuses his attention on the national fair, theatre entertainment, and the aesthetics of Russian Middle Ages, while Larionov reacts to what we would call now "city kitsch," mostly in its European and provocative fauvist version. A still life by Rozhdestvenski is a movement towards a new stage in the development of some "Jacks" when they were mostly attracted to the paintings of Cezanne. Falk's *Self Portrait* (1923) is both Cezannism and at the same time something very historical: his psychology with some traces of symbolism makes us think of certain European masters of the 17th century. In the year of the five-year jubilee there was opposition to the pathos of the emerging "socialist realism" by those groups of young artists who demonstrated loyalty to the Soviet regime by using the themes of life and revolutionary Russia and rendering them with great optimism.

Konchalovski's *Floor-Polisher* is unique. It is connected with the neo-classical utopia that was extremely important for the "Jacks" and Cezannists in the1920s through common sense and free dialogue. Due to a somewhat provocative decorative factor, this large-scale sketch is reminiscent of the bold experiments of the Russian pre-avant-garde and the fauvists. And, in general, the work of this 70-year old master has nothing to do with the socialist realism ideology. The painting exudes a love of freedom and hope for the future

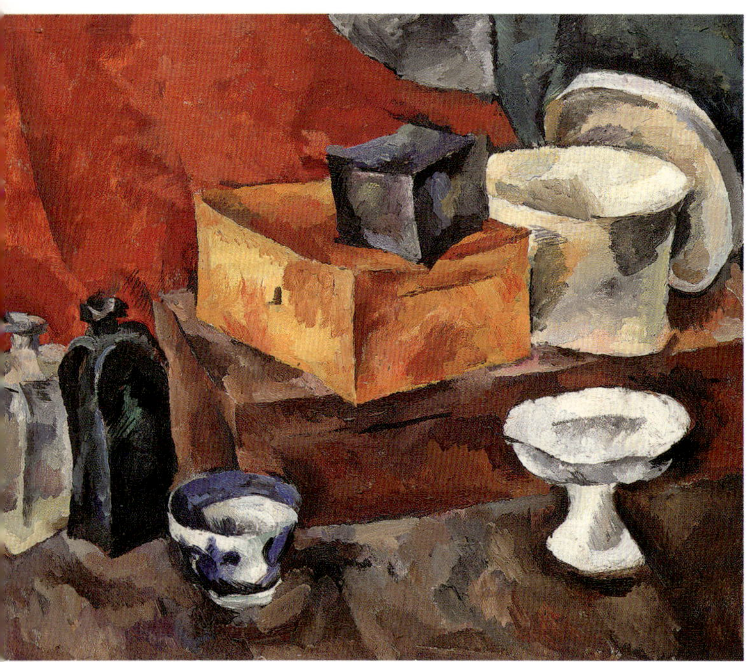

Piotr KONCHALOVSKI. **Still-Life.** 1911
Oil on canvas. 41¾ x 51½ in. (107 x 132 cm)

as well as illusions of emotional enthusiasm that was so evident then, in the very beginning of the Second World War, when one could hardly imagine that Stalin's later repression and the beginning of the Cold War would soon change world history. This painting by Konchalovski is timeless and universal. It is an indicator of a renovation (though soon artificially neutralized) that would be taken by young artists of the 1950s and 1960s.

An interesting fact: while Stalinist critics of the late 1940s fought against "impressionism" and "naturalistically tiny themes," thus threatening the development of the realistic genre and landscape genre, it was these two genres that returned as the most important artistic phenomena in the period of The Thaw. Small, simple landscape paintings were the direct opposites of officially standardized canvases depicting the heroes of the Soviet way of life. At the same time, a strong artistic gust of fresh air arrived after Stalin's death and made these small pictures look far brighter and more dynamic. Their arrival coincided with the rehabilitation in post-Stalin Russia, with French impressionism again shining from the walls of state museums. The tendency strengthened the positions of lyrical landscape painters of the oldest generation, such as M. Romadin, as well as the young V. Stozharov, A. and S. Tkachev, I. Sorokin, and others. Their early works, full of freshness, are presented at this exhibition.

Socialist realism, as it was officially seen and recognized in the USSR, was not just realism "Made in Russia." Obviously it was to be a kind of art easily understandable by any "simple" viewer, that is to say truthful and realistic. But on such canvases the artists were to depict some ideal reality, a life that had not yet emerged, but which would appear in the near future, according to the communist ideology. The depiction of a communist "heaven" was closely connected with the ideology because it was one of the means of the communist reconstruction of reality. A new generation of Soviet people was to have been born in accordance with the positive examples provided by the socialist artists. Such an artist would have demonstrated his loyalty to the Communist Party and kept to the political imperatives of the moment as defined by the leaders of the state.

That is why in practice socialist realism is not always equal to itself. It had certain (sanctioned by officials) modifications in the 1930s, 1940s and early 1950s. In the late Soviet years there appeared a so-called "final model" of socialist realism that can be named Brezhnev's socialist realism. At every stage, politically urgent issues were selected and arranged in a hierarchy, according to the priorities of the officials. Historical and revolutionary issues were the highest priorities. Some artists called these "the issues of the Chief." Below these was the issue of the Red Army. Next was the issue of labor, demonstrating the major achievements of socialist realism. At the lowest stage were the idealized personifications of Soviet life, images of the Soviet New Man and the Soviet New Woman. In formal interpretations, this art preferred academic truth of depiction to true realism. Though at its early stages socialist realism provided more romance and sincerity, at that time true illusions of the new political system were much stronger. Later its images became more and more structured and were filled with ritual solemnity on which the whole body of official political propaganda was orientated.

Among the generally recognized artists in this exhibition are Aleksandr Gerasimov, Boris Yakovlev, Aleksandr Deineka, and their younger colleagues from the USSR Academy of Arts, Vasili Nechitailo and Geli Korzhev. But it is not their official "hits" that are on display here, though perhaps Yakovlev will surprise viewers with his painting praising Soviet efficiency, *Soviet Canned Food*. It was commissioned by the Soviet government for a well-known exhibition, "Industry of Socialist Realism" (1939), as a testament to the outstanding success of the Soviet food industry. A. Gerasimov, Stalin's favorite artist and a talented master, is represented with a landscape depicting a flourishing garden, demonstrating that he received his training from a decorative and impressionist school of painting. Nechitailo and Korzhev are shown as the creators of nudes, paintings that were officially condemned. (Remember: the ideologists of Soviet morals proclaimed that in the USSR there was no sex.) But still, such paintings were produced in the USSR, though not for official exhibitions, but for the artists themselves. Remaining hidden to the general public, it was often these particular works that revealed the original elements in the work of an individual artist. These people lived double lives: for the "bosses" (for the "people") and for themselves, their peers, and for how they saw art in general. Such a phenomenon was a commonplace practice in the Soviet Union. Personal aesthetic passions could not provide an artist with any solid professional and social status within a totalitarian system.

A movement of young artists opposed to the official dictates of socialist realism was widening and strengthening in the 1960s. On the one hand, they sought to reveal the true drama of the Soviet reality, rejecting its false depiction. On the other hand, they were seriously searching for authentic cultural values, spirit, morals and national traditions instead of propagandist dogmas of the state. Examples of these tendencies are evidenced in the severe style painting, *Remembering: Widows*, by Viktor Popkov who died tragically at a very young age similarly to Vladimir Vysozky or Vasili Shukshin, and the light and positive world of the *Young Family* by Dmitri Zhilinski. These talented artists appeal to aesthetic and ethic ideals of Russian iconography and the early Renaissance. But notice that none of these phenomena fit the socialist realism patterns. Such links to the past were at that time one of the ways to renew and liberate the spirit. A tendency that opposed Culture in favor of semi- and pseudo-culture was typical for the period and was always relentlessly pursued by the officials.

Finally, I would like you to consider the landscape art of Sergei Gerasimov. (Please don't confuse him with A. Gerasimov, who in many aspects was very different). His masterpiece, *Evening*, is from the collection of The Museum of Russian Art. It is the close partnership with this museum and its founder, Mr. Raymond E. Johnson that led to the realization of this exhibition.

Sergei Gerasimov continued the traditions of the Moscow school of painting. In his youth, these traditions had dominated such outstanding personalities as K. Korovin and V. Serov. And, generally speaking, Gerasimov inherited Serov's understanding of the sense and virtual system of landscape painting. But the process of building fluidity into in his art is very different from the methods of the Moscow school of the period. The teachers and their students treated paint in different ways. Though he didn't belong to the avant-garde movement, S. Gerasimov nevertheless, was highly influenced by the Russian modernism of the

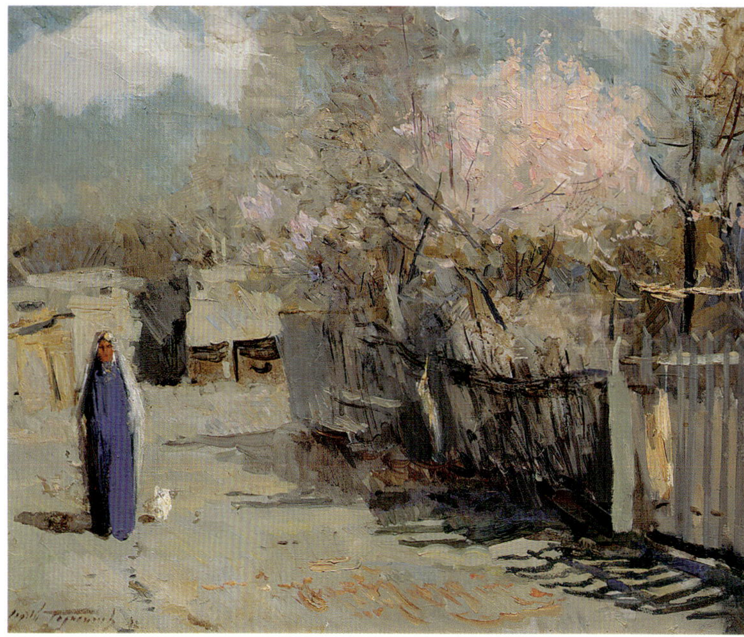

Sergei GERASIMOV. **Spring. Trees in Blossom. Samarkand.** 1942
Oil on canvas. 21 x 34¾ in. (69 x 89 cm)

1910s and 1920s. His landscape style is quite paradoxical. The composition is established by only a few calm colors and tones that render the image mainly contemplative. But what he does with each one of these colors and tones! The brush moves energetically, often sharply, with maximum nervous energy, and a complete world appears to be ready to burst from within the chaos of brush strokes, interrupted, short and long.

This technique can be called the psychological authenticity of the modern feeling of nature. It is presented in all of Gerasimov's best landscapes, and it is the lively basis of his realistic stylistics. Within the Russian context Gerasimov's art is very important. First, his artistic model was thoroughly worked through and reflected upon; it was his reason for living. (This was properly understood by his contemporaries.) Sergei Gerasimov discovered this mature concept toward the end of the 1920s and into the 1930s, and he developed it through the early 1960s, that is, until the end of his life. Although he was "punished"– he was replaced as director of the Moscow Artistic Institute named after Surikov– it was during the 1940s and the early 1950s that he influenced young Russian artists to the greatest extent. In fact, he was one of the greatest teachers of the generation of artists responsible for the artistic Thaw in the late 1950s and early 1960s. Through his teachings, he demonstrated that Russian realism, first of all, is a type of artistic mentality, rather than a loyalty to some rigid style formulas that were established somewhere in the past.

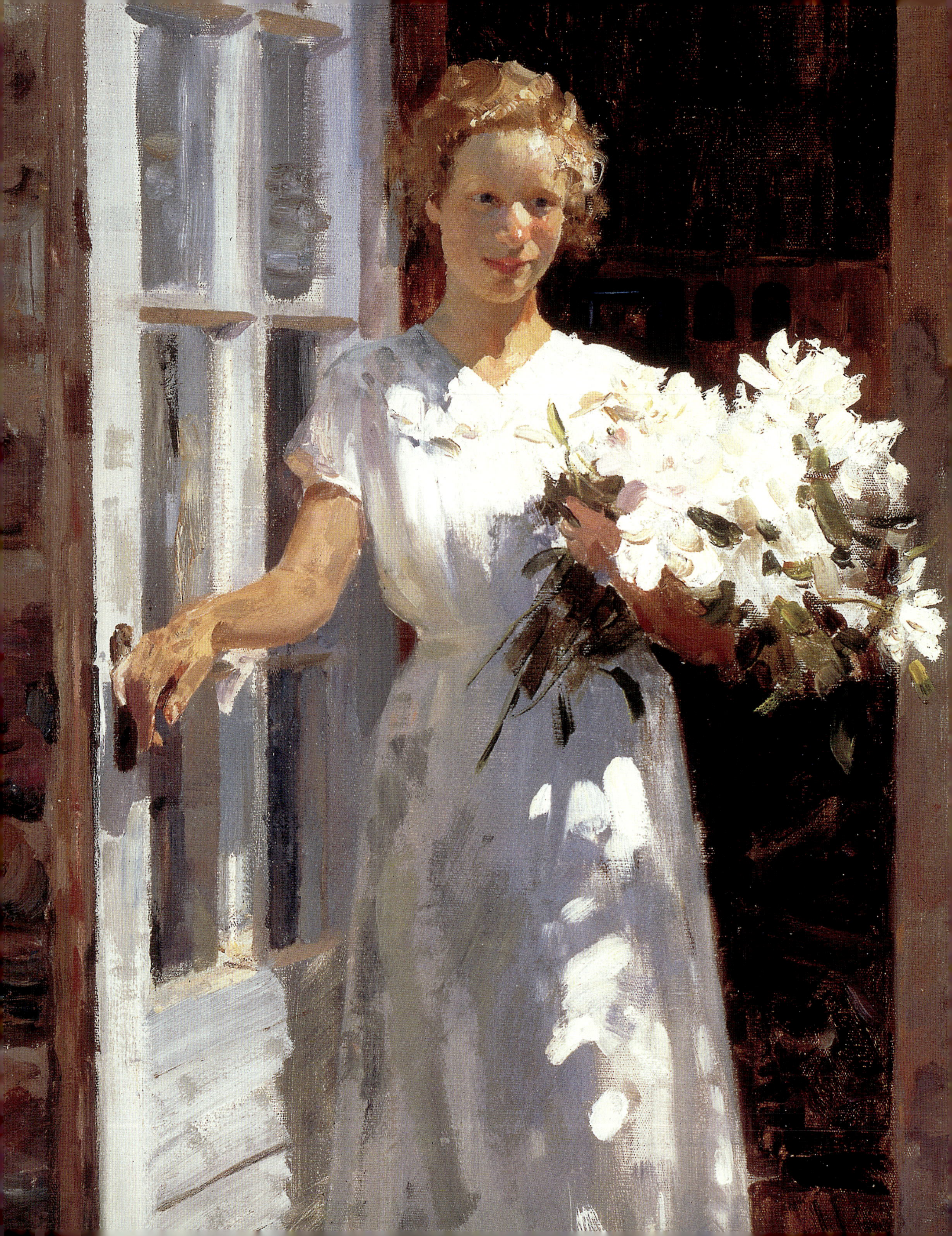

A Century of Russian Art

John Bowlt

Redefining History

The exhibition "In the Russian Tradition" touches on many important issues. Here are paintings by artists, both celebrated and unfamiliar, that cannot be accommodated readily within the conventional perimeters that the academy, the marketplace, and political ideology have imposed upon the history of Russian art. After all, most Western viewers now associate 20th century Russian art exclusively with the radical innovations of the avant-garde, the triumphant rhetoric of the Stalin style, the iconoclasm of the dissident movement, and today the brash experiments in video, performance and installation.

Certainly, all these manifestations form a legitimate part of the development of modern Russian art and have every right to be examined in detail. But "In the Russian Tradition" tells us that Russian--and Soviet – art is much more than the sum total of such general conventions: here are works of art such as Yuri Pimenov's *Chinese Theater* and Sergei Gerasimov's *Evening* that fall outside accepted categories such as "avant-garde" and Socialist Realism, but that still stress and maintain the reportorial impetus of Russian culture as a whole. Ultimately, they may constitute a tradition alternative to the esthetic canon that majority decision has imposed upon us. After all, who is to say that in the grand scheme of things Aleksandr Rodchenko was superior to Vasili Efanov or that Kuzma Petrov-Vodkin was less influential than Vasili Kandinsky? "In the Russian Tradition" presents us with a century of original and engaging artworks that, curiously enough and refreshingly so, have little in common with the canonical vocabulary of Kazimir Malevich's *Black Square*, Vladimir Tatlin's *Monument to the III International*, Stalin's architectural wedding cakes or in our own time Ilya Kabakov's provocative interiors. How can the force of these discrepant and deviant models–this other tradition–be explained?

The Legacy of Realism

"In the Russian Tradition" invites the viewer to associate works such as Leonid Kabachek's *On the Way* or Georgi Nisski's *Moscow Suburbs, February* not with the strident abstract legacy of the 1910s or the utopias of the Constructivist revolution, but with the ample tradition of 19th century Realism as represented, for example, by Ilya Repin's *Portrait of V.V. Stasov* and Valentin Serov's *Portrait of Mika Morozov.* Repin, Serov, and their colleagues (not least, the writer Lev Tolstoy) identified the primary function of art as a didactic or, at least, narrative one and they offered their depictions of people and places, palpable and recognizable, as pictorial extensions of a concrete, material world. It is this conception of art, tendentious, declarative, and physical, that persisted throughout the 20th century and informed painters as diverse as Eduard Bragovsky and Aleksandr Osmerkin, Semon Rotnitski and Tair Salakhov.

All this is to say that respect of the Realist or, at least, narrative, tradition remained exceptionally strong throughout the 20th century, leaving a deep imprint upon movements and associations active both before and after the Revolution of October, 1917. Among the early and influential groups were the Union of Russian Artists, the Jack of Diamonds, and the Society of Studio Artists (OST), with which, variously, several of the artists here were connected: as contributors to the Union of Russian Artists, Petrov-Vodkin provided a Symbolist interpretation of the Apocalypse (*The Bathing of the Red Horse*), Filipp Malyavin evinced the primitive energy of the peasant (*Village Girl*), and Konstantin Yuon explored the legacy of Russian Orthodoxy (*Annunciation Day*); as members of the Jack of Diamonds, Robert Falk, Petr Konchalovski, Mikhail Larionov, and Vasili Rozhdestvenski emphasized the tactility of people and things (*Self-Portrait, Floor-Polisher, Prostitute at the*

Konstantin MAKSIMOV. **Graduate**. 1960. Detail
Oil on canvas. 39 x 25 in. (99 x 64 cm)

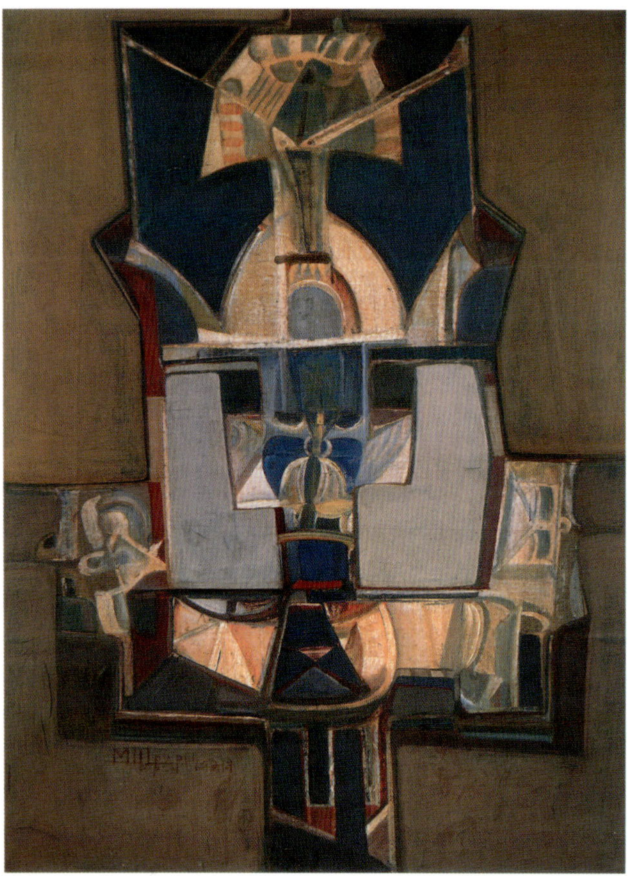

Mikhail SHVARTSMAN. **Formula of Dolphin.** 1978
Tempera on panel. 29¼ x 39 in. (75 x 100 cm)

Hairdresser's, Still Life with Green Bottle); and as prominent supporters of OST in the 1920s, Aleksandr Deineka, Yuri Pimenov, and Petr Williams often resorted to an unsettling Expressionist distortion in their visions of early Soviet reality (*Girl Sitting on a Chair, Chinese Theater, Nana*).

Not surprisingly, the primary Socialist Realists of the Stalin era such as Aleksandr Gerasimov (*Trees in Bloom*), Igor Grabar (*Snows of March*), and Efanov (*Marinka*) drew upon these precedents as did their more impressionistic disciples such as Vladimir Gavrilov (*A Fresh Day*) and Aleksei Gritsai (*Blue Shadows: Msta River*). In turn, the followers of the so called Severe Style in the 1970s such as Geli Korzhev-Chuvelev (*Marusya*) and Salakhov (*Aidan*) and even the intrepid explorers of formulae at stylistic loggerheads with ideological demand such as Dmitri Zhilinski (*Young Families*) and Viktor Popkov (*Remembering: Widows*) still emphasized the narrative function of painting. Last, but not least, the fact that Naum Gabo, Pavel Filonov, Vasili Kandinsky, Mikhail Larionov, and Malevich, pillars of the avant-garde, all used the word "Realist" to describe their deviant systems is also symptomatic of the constancy of this Russian cultural bias – and of the weight, if not perhaps of 19th century Realism, then of the Orthodox word and the Imperial decree.

The Persistence of Memory

The preeminence of the term and concept "Realism" in Russia's artistic vocabulary, even during the heyday of extreme movements such as Rayism, Suprematism, and Constructivism which ostensibly, rejected the illusionistic and documentary function of art gives pause for thought. Certainly, if, for example, in 1915 Malevich referred to his abstract system as a "new painterly Realism" and in 1920 Gabo to his constructions as "Realist," perhaps we should ask ourselves why they did so. On the one hand, such artists may have been maintaining the philosophical journey of the Symbolists *ab realia ad realiora* and identifying an abstract, higher state of consciousness as "more real;" on the other hand, however, they were still very close in time to the Positivism of the late 19th century, they grew up in the shadow of Repin and Tolstoy, and the swiftness and abruptness with which they rejected the Realist tradition may indicate proximity and familiarity rather than distance and distaste.

Take the banquet year of 1910, for example, which saw the opening of the "Jack of Diamonds" exhibition in Moscow, a milestone in the history of the Russian avant-garde and the individual careers of Kandinsky, Larionov, Malevich, and many other radicals. Most histories of Russian art devote substantial coverage to this episode, identifying it as a vital moment in the consolidation of avant-garde forces. While the importance of such developments cannot be denied, it should also be remembered that 1910 witnessed the flowering not only of other radical associations such as the Union of Youth in St. Petersburg, but also of more moderate, traditional societies which carried forward the banner of Realism until well after the October Revolution. Chief among these was the Union of Russian Artists and the World of Art, in which several of the artists in this exhibition (Grabar and Yuon, for example) played formative roles both as exhibitors and as administrators. Although both of these groups ended their formal activities in the early 1920s, they left a strong imprint on the first generation of Soviet artists, prompting them to question the leftist dictatorship of the avant-garde and to develop a simpler style–a Proletarian Realism–that, allegedly, would be more appropriate to the needs of the masses. Under the auspices of the Association of Artists of Revolutionary Russia (AKhRR), founded in 1922, the champions of what was then called Heroic Realism such as Aleksandr Gerasimov, Sergei Gerasimov (not related), and Vasili Yakovlev elaborated a style that both drew upon the

Russian tradition (encapsulated in Repin's and Serov's paintings) and projected "not abstract concoctions, but a true picture of events".

Be that as it may, the Bolshevik Revolution of October, 1917, which affected all walks of cultural life, tends to be connected with the accomplishments of the artistic left rather than of the right. On the one hand, the political and social insurrection undermined or transformed existing artistic institutions and establishments, and, on the other, it energized the radical trends, prompting many of the avant-garde painters and sculptors to assume positions of ideological, bureaucratic, and pedagogical privilege. This politicized welcome to artists such as Kandinsky, Malevich, Rodchenko and Tatlin can be explained by many circumstances, but, of particular significance is the fact that, initially, some of the leftists regarded their radical art as a logical counterpart to Lenin's radical politics and offered their systems to the service of the state. In turn, the Party rewarded them with government commissions, teaching and research positions in art schools and think tanks, and ready access to exhibitions and publications. This happy coincidence of conditions meant that many artists derived immediate artistic and material benefit from the new regime, something that led to a robust, if short-lived, dictatorship of the left, especially in Moscow.

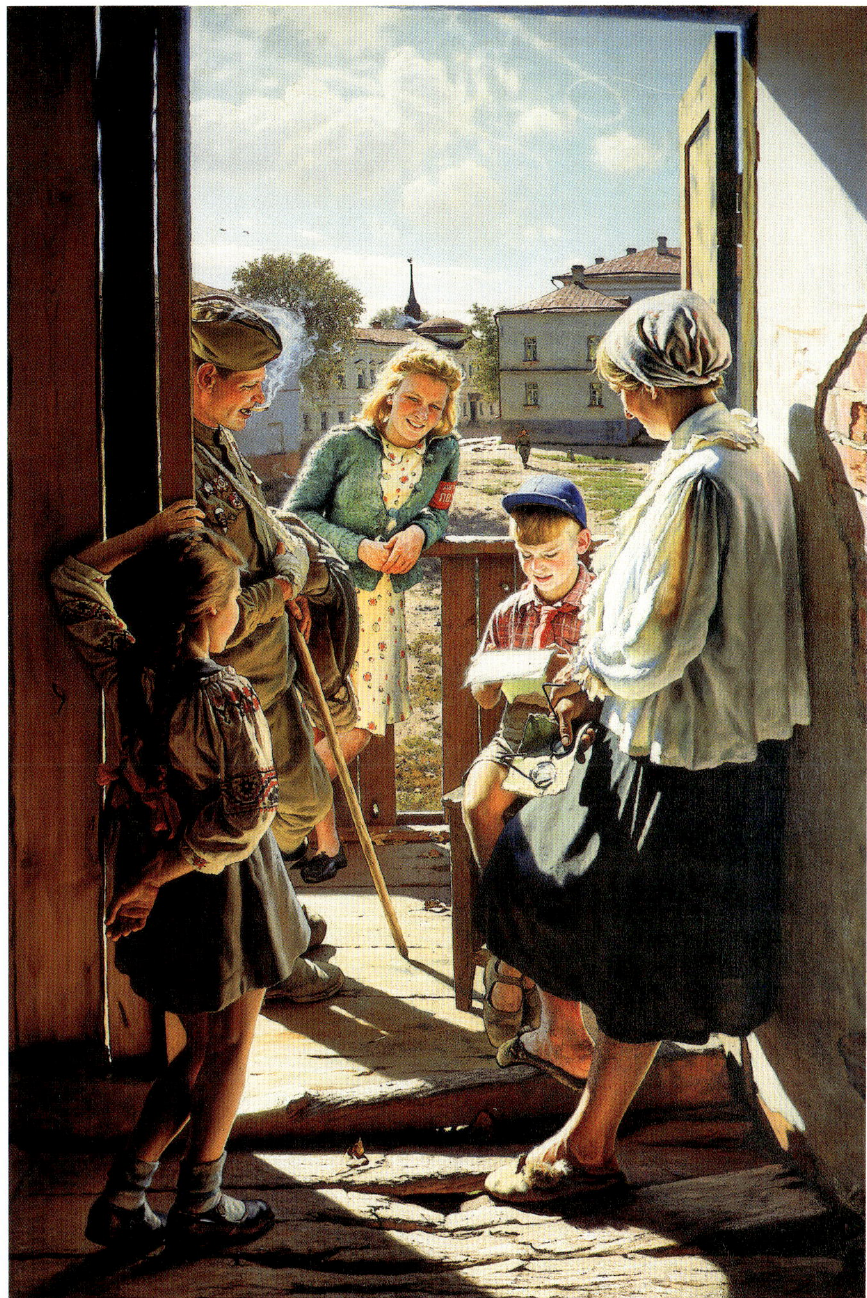

Aleksandr LAKTIONOV. **Letter from the Front.** 1947
Oil on canvas. 87¾ x 60½ in. (225 x 155 cm)

However, the predicament of Russian art just after the Revolution was by no means simple or uniform. If there was a leftist dictatorship, it was momentary, flawed, and disunited, and its potential was undermined by inner disagreement, ideological defection, and then emigration (Kandinsky leaving in 1921, for example). Moreover, what is often forgotten in this context is that the "right" was also active in matters of culture, that, from the very first, the new masses preferred Realism to abstract art, and that the more moderate painters such as Grabar, Konchalovsky, Arkadi Rylov and Yuon were also convinced that the Revolution needed recognizable imagery and simple narratives. Some of them took up important positions in the new cultural hierarchy (Grabar in the Tretyakov Gallery, Rozhdestvenski in the reformed teaching system, Yuon in the Russian Academy of Artistic Sciences), endeavoring to rescue, refurbish, and propagate the highest traditions of the past. Lenin, incidentally, sympathized far more with their activities than with the enigmas of the avant-garde, welcoming the new Realism of AKhRR and

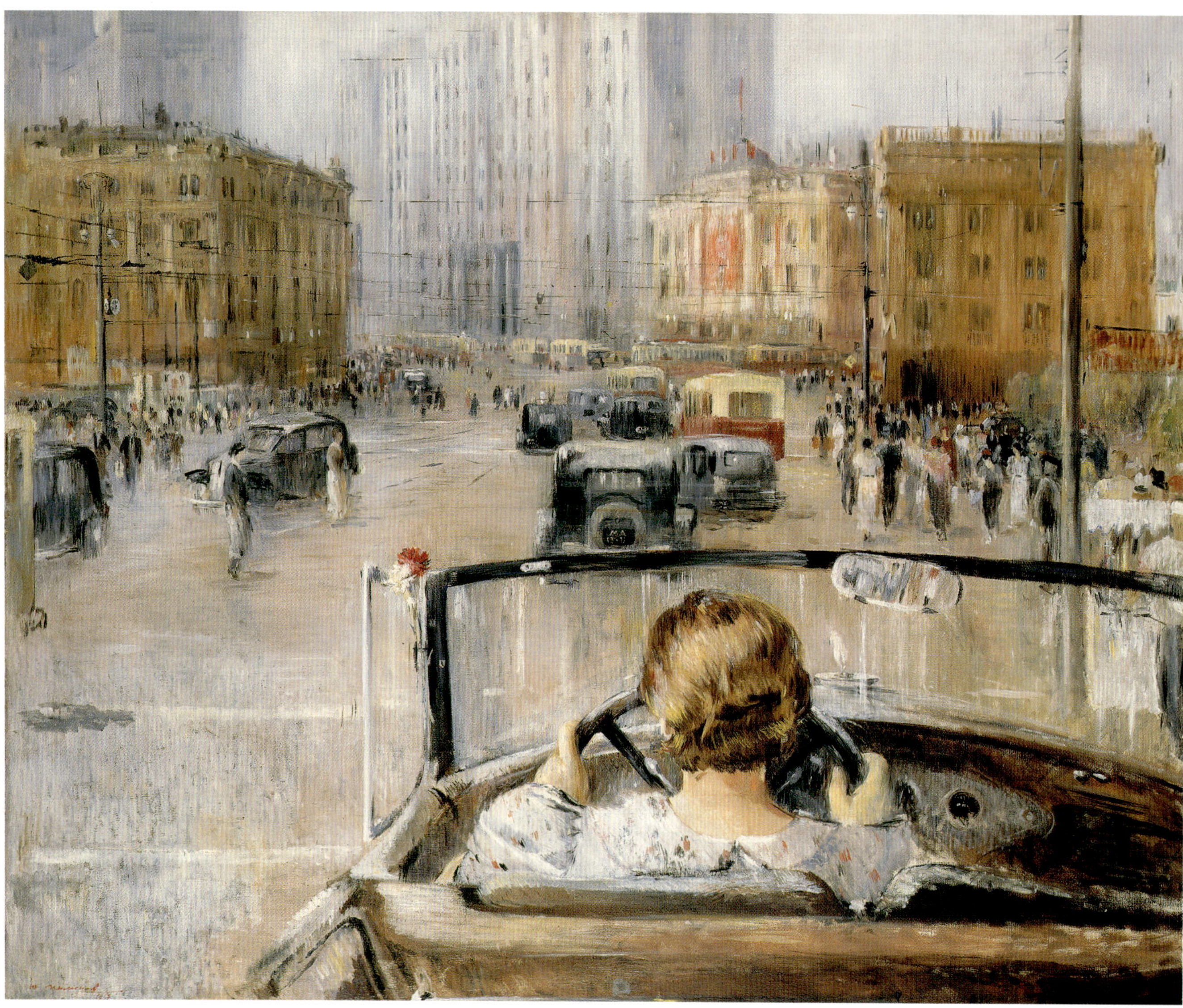

Yuri PIMENOV. **The New Moscow**. 1937. Oil on canvas. 54⅞ x 66¼ in. (140 x 170 cm)

emphasizing the ideological relevance of Repin and Tolstoy.

True, in the 1920s AKhRR was not the only group that claimed primacy as the inventor of an essential Soviet style, its arch rival, OST, for example, still acknowledging the formal inventions of the avant-garde–as is manifest in the early, experimental work of Deineka and Pimenov. However, AKhRR gained increasing momentum, appealing both to the political demands of the Party apparatus and to the unpretentious taste of the working-classes, and its portraits of leaders such as Mikhail Frunze, Lenin, and Kliment Voroshilov, pictures of factory and farm, and rousing scenes of war and revolution provided a strong visual basis for the formulation of Socialist Realism in the early 1930s–the monolithic esthetic canon that guided all aspects of Soviet culture until the 1980s.

Socialist Realism

Bearing in mind the didactic bias of Russian and Soviet painting, it is in keeping that the principles of Socialist Realism were explicated and advanced primarily in terms of literature–at the First Congress of Soviet Writers in Moscow in 1934.

At that international gathering Maksim Gorky, the father of Soviet letters, Andrei Zhdanov, Secretary of the Communist Party of the Soviet Union, and other luminaries identified concepts such as "typicality," "Party spirit," and "revolutionary Romanticism" as being fundamental to the new style. Their assumptions were supported by representatives of other disciplines, including Grabar, who spoke on behalf of the visual arts.

The influence of the Congress on the development of Soviet culture was dramatic. With the ratifica-

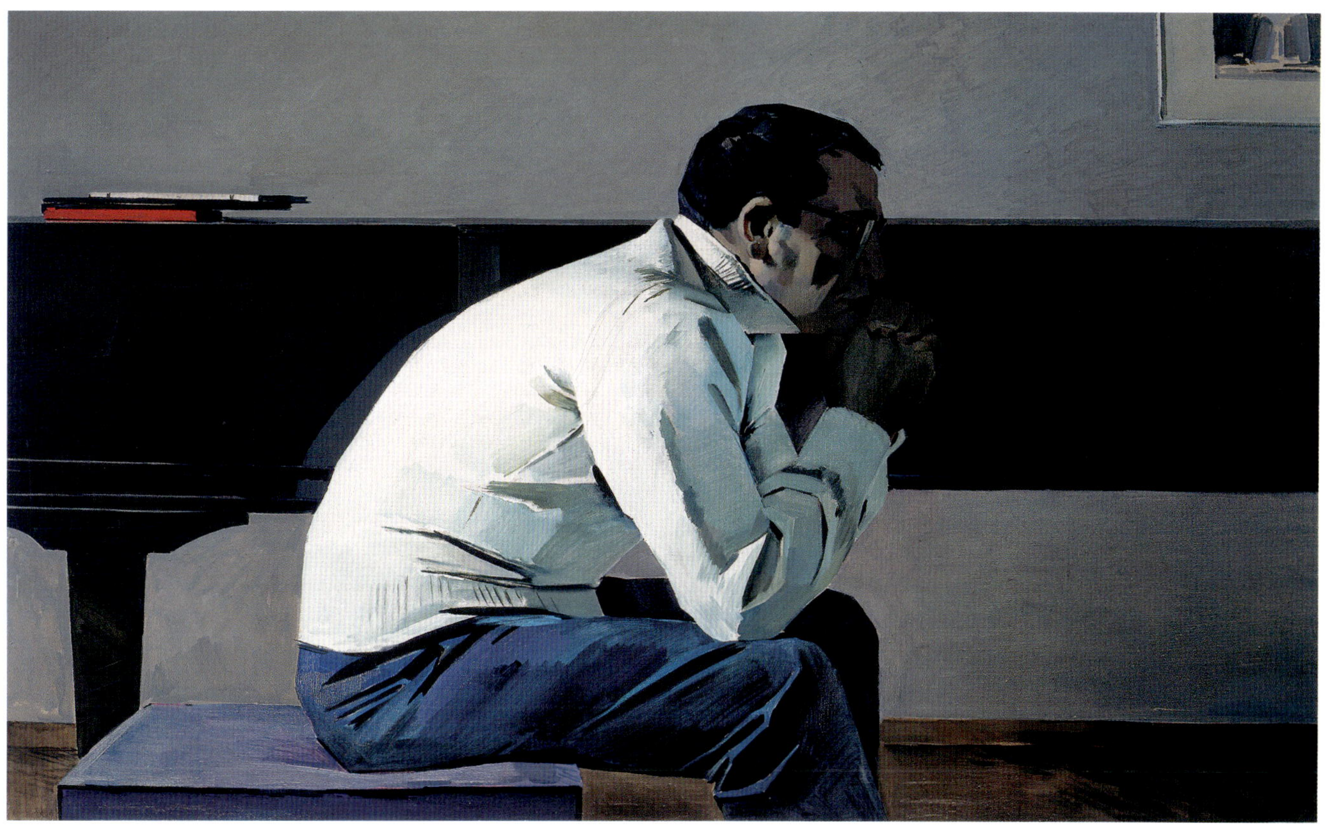

Tair SALAKHOV. **Portrait of Composer Kara Karaev**. 1960. Oil on canvas. 47¼ x 79¾ in. (121 x 203 cm)

tion of Socialist Realism as "national in form, Socialist in content" and the subsequent, continual condemnations of "Formalism" and "bourgeois art," the Soviet literary, visual, and performing arts soon developed in close collaboration with the seats of political and financial power–the Academy of Arts, the Union of Artists of the USSR, and the Ministry of Culture. Yet Stalin himself seemed little excited by painting and sculpture, making scant reference to them in his speeches and writings, even if sycophants did credit him with inventing the term Socialist Realism, a "definition of genius".

In spite of rigorous supervision at all levels, the style of Socialist Realism was not entirely static and, as with any esthetic premise, its basic presuppositions were open to a degree of interpretation – even exhortations such as "working on the image of Stalin is the embodiment of the basic, central theme of Socialist Realism." At the same time, dismissal of the values of the Russian avant-garde and of much contemporary European and American art meant that Soviet artists were denied exposure to alternative systems. Even artists of the older generation who had worked, broadly speaking, within the sidelines of Realism such as Deineka, Falk, and Petrov-Vodkin were still criticized for their alienation from the Soviet system. Sometimes the very champions of Socialist Realism such as S. Gerasimov and Nisski fell victim to the Party watchdogs for an alleged interest in French Impressionism, a precedence of form over content, an indistinct ideological message, etc.

During the Second World War many Soviet artists were mobilized to serve as battle-painters, to make action sketches for newspapers and magazines, and even to paint camouflage. Direct encounters with the front line led to the consolidation of the so-called thematic picture–visual accounts of real incidents rather than metaphorical interpretations for which Deineka, Efanov, and Vasili Nechitailo, in particular, should be remembered. Painters who had been content to depict innocuous landscapes or family scenes were now expected to emphasize patriotic values: in his *Mother of a Partisan* (1943, Tretyakov Gallery), for example, S. Gerasimov, turned from the tranquility of his sunsets to poignant praise of individual sacrifice, while Arkadi Plastov used the simple Russian landscape to expose the cruelty of war as in *A Fascist Flew Past* (1942, Tretyakov Gallery). Similarly, the celebrated Kukryniksy trio (Mikhail Kuprianov, Porfiri Krylov, and Nikolai Sokolov) also oriented their talents towards topical easel paintings as they continued to produce trenchant caricatures and cartoons. The tragedy of the Second World War remained a princi-

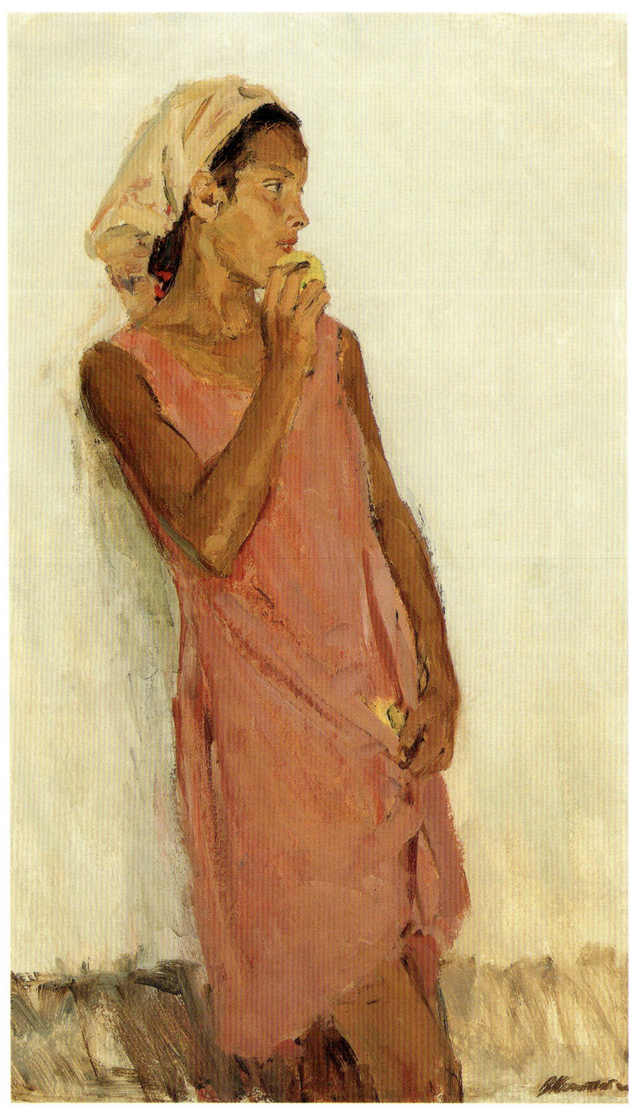

Vasili K. NECHITAILO. **Girl with an Apple.** Mid 1950s. Oil on board. 27¼ x 16¾ IN. (70 x 43 cm)

pal subject long after the defeat of Germany, and Soviet artists chose it not necessarily because of political exigency and professional ambition, but in genuine homage to the fallen. Viktor Popkov's *Widows. Remembering* is a moving example of this sincerity and commitment.

Breaking the Mold

With Stalin's death in 1953 and Khrushchev's Secret Speech of 1956 Soviet culture entered a period of enquiry and adjustment known as the Thaw. Guardedly and ever subject to Party control, the Soviet public learned about alternative literary and artistic styles through translations of Western prose and poetry, publications on French Impressionism, even international exhibitions of contemporary art. One result of this cultural exposure was the emergence of a new and dynamic group of writers and artists who questioned the validity of Socialist Realism, among them the poet Evgeni Evtushenko, the painter Ilya Glazunov, and the sculptor Ernst Neizvestny. Like the Russian Realists a century before them, these angry young men dared to criticize, to parody, and to experiment, while still advocating, incidentally, the need for art to communicate and convert. Here were dissident voices loud and clear, refreshing and potential in what had been a virtual desert of esthetic innovation.

But the interval of optimism was brief and an open conflict between the "official" and the "unofficial" artists took place in December, 1962, at the exhibition "Thirty Years of Moscow Art" held at the Manege in Moscow. The panorama included both veteran artists who still occupied an ambivalent position in the Soviet pantheon such as Falk and David Shterenberg and young painters and sculptors who, in their experimental works, were challenging the canon of Socialist Realism. So upset was Khrushchev with these digressions that he called for a reinforcement of the Party's position in matters of culture, exclaiming to his recalcitrant audience, "Gentlemen, we are declaring war on you!" The campaign did, indeed, last many years, resulting in the arrest, imprisonment, and mass emigration of many underground artists and writers. But the movement never lost momentum, advancing the dissident cause through *samizdat* writings, apartment exhibitions, unsanctioned performances, and Western publicity.

The counterpoint of "official" vs. "unofficial" that characterized much of late Soviet culture is an exceptionally complex subject. If there were artists and writers who did represent the bastion of Party power (e.g. A. Gerasimov) and unrelenting dissidents who challenged that power (e.g. Aleksandr Solzhenitsyn), there were many individuals who felt no strong commitment to either camp. The varied contributions to "In the Russian Tradition" indicate that in some sense the Soviet–and Russian–style evolved outside and in spite of these factions and that its achievements can often be measured and assessed independently of the ideological machine. Of course, it might be argued that some artists such as Yuri Katts, Rotnitski, and Sergei Tutunov, reluctant to follow the Party line, simply turned inwards, painting apolitical scenes such as the Classical still life or the Russian winter. Refusing to accept banal commissions or to compromise their own vision, such artists became internal emigres.

This does not mean that the essential impetus of Socialist Realism or, rather, the many interpretations that distinguished the Khrushchev and Brezhnev eras, ceased to attract artistic forces. Certainly, primacy of place should be given to the non-conformists as fighters for artistic license, but, on the other hand, to disregard the later stages of Socialist Realism would be to distort the history of modern Russian art. After all, many of the artists at "In the Russian Tradition" were not vociferous dissidents, accepted everyday Soviet life as their subject, and moved easily within the perimeters of the official stylistic and thematic repertoires. The noble values of social equality, industrial development, united family, agricultural abundance, children's health, and hard work, promoted as essential to the implementation of Communism, return in many of the pictures here. Whether these values are credible or mythical, whether painters such as Nikolai Baskakov with his happy milkmaids, Zinaida Kovalevskaya with her ethnic gatherers of tomatoes or Popkov with his serene family in July were earnest or not is now perhaps less substantive than the existence of the paintings themselves. We are left with captivating images which, like all historical documents, tell the truth, but not the whole truth.

Painters such as the Tkachev brothers (*Post Girl in Winter*), Eduard Bagrovsky (*Logging on the Vetluga*), and Oleg Lomakin (*Road Worker: Nina*) were among those committed to the Realist idea, even if they tended to present their visions of workers, industrial projects, and new apartments through an Impressionist lens or with a manifest homage to the severity of German Expressionism as mediated by their elders, Deineka and Pimenov (Salakhov's *Aidan* is a case in point). Similarly, "In the Russian Tradition" includes paintings that capture and convince more by understatement and restraint rather than by rhetoric and glamour: Pimenov's *Waiting* reminds us of the unheeding bureaucracy and endless lines in offices and stores during the Brezhnev era, Gritsai's *Blue Shadows* of the humility of the local countryside, Vladimir Stozharov's *Novgorod. Yaroslav Monastery* of the hieratic majesty of Russia's past, Igor Popov's *Our Courtyard* of the simple pleasures of skiing, playing, and gossiping in the snow.

Looking Back

The exhibition "In the Russian Tradition" is a summary of past accomplishment rather than a suggestion of potential experiment and the constituent paintings belong to an epoch fast fading into history. Of course, some would argue that the Russian tradition, especially the Realist esthetic, is still strong, commands popular support, and can resist the provocations of the new avant-garde. Indeed, it would be reassuring to accept that point of view: "In the Russian Tradition" teaches us not only to respect intrinsic tradition, but also, in so doing, to rediscover a forgotten lineage of modern Russian art and to realize that Soviet Socialist Realism carried nuances and subtleties that have often been overlooked. "In the Russian Tradition" redistributes esthetic weights and measures, challenges the historiographical hegemony of the avant-garde and of the Stalin style, and forces us to retell the story of Russian art. At its highest level, Soviet Socialist Realism engages by its sheer technical bravura (cf. Korzhev-Chuvelev's *Morning* or Yakovlev's *Soviet Canned Food*) reminiscent of the 19th century Academy; but it can also engender a disturbing sensuality (Gavrilov's *A Fresh Day*) and a pregnant mystery (Pimenov's *Waiting*) and can even make us believe momentarily in the ideals of an alternative social system. But in a global society that treasures instantaneity, noise, mechanical perfection, and violence, the pictures at "In the Russian Tradition" also constitute a nostalgic voyage to a distant world where ideological belief, political order, and cultural awareness seemed to be fashioning a radiant future. But as we peer back through the gloom of history and try to distinguish fact from fiction, we may also conclude that "In the Russian Tradition" describes a reality that existed only in the pictures that we see before us.

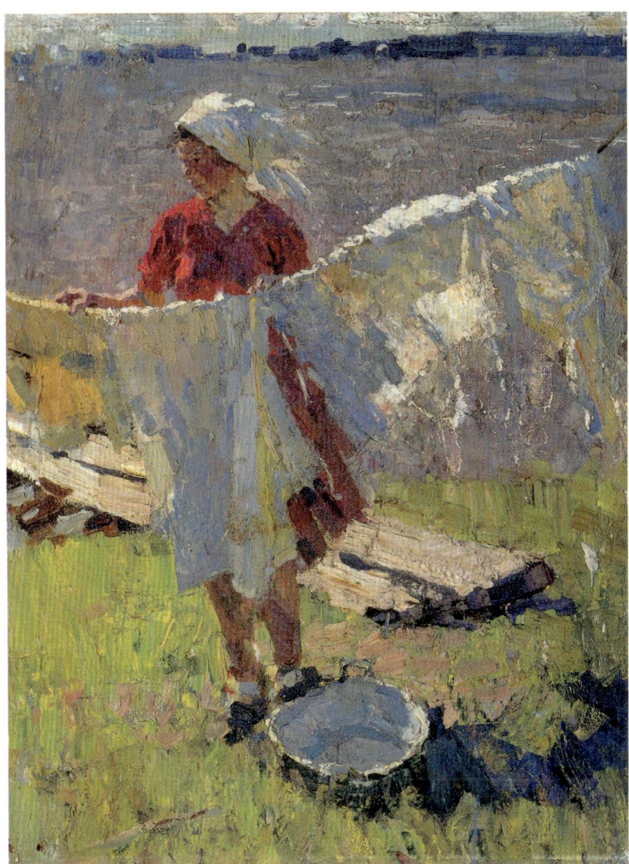

Sergei TKACHEV. **Windy Day.** 1957. Oil on canvas. 21⅝ x 17½ in. (58 x 45 cm)

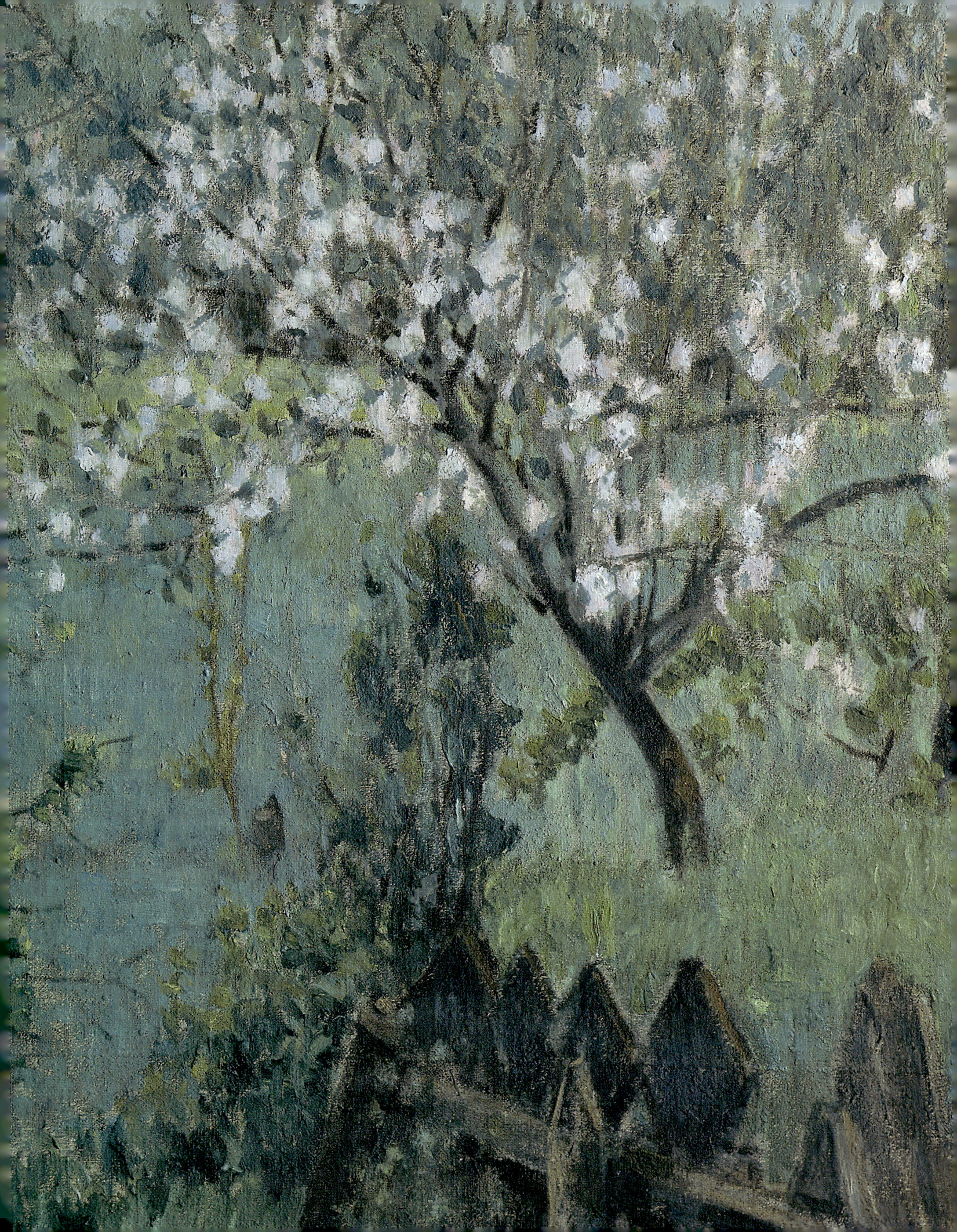

In the Russian Tradition

Maria Bulanova

The exhibition, "In the Russian Tradition," does not seek to thoroughly demonstrate all traditions in Russian art of the 20th century. What you see is only a portion of what, on the one hand can seem very familiar, but on the other, absolutely unknown to the Westerner. Here are works of the "official artists" of the Soviet era who are known in the West as "politically engaged." The representatives of the phenomenon conventionally named "official Soviet art" were Vladimir Stozharov, Vasili Nechitailo, Sergei and Aleksei Tkachev, Igor Popov, Sergei Gerasimov, Aleksei Gerasimov, Aleksandr Deineka, Yuri Pimenov, Boris Yakovlev, Nikolai Romadin, Victor Popkov, Petr Konchalovski and many others whose paintings hang side by side with those by such renowned Russian masters as Ilya Repin, Valentin Serov and even Aristarkh Lentulov and Mikhail Larionov. What prompted us to unite within one exhibition these artistic concepts which are often considered so different from one another? The answer is this: our search for justice and a strong desire to be objective.

The 20th century came to an end very recently, but already we have begun to distance ourselves from it, both politically and historically. Of course, we are not able to achieve complete distance–life and art are too tightly knit, too closely related. And in no way do we wish to forget the tragedies that Russia endured in the 20th century: numerous revolutions, a civil war, two world wars that claimed millions of lives, a long lasting communist regime and so on–we cannot discount it, nor do we seek to ignore it.

In presenting this exhibition we are displaying the art form called socialist realism not from the point of view that it was an exotic style of the Soviet empire, the function of which was to promote communist policies. On the contrary, we would argue from the approach that "socialist realism" is limited to politics. We believe that the natural inner development of Russian art had its origins outside of the political context. In the opinion of the exhibition organizers, Russian art is a part of the world's modernist cultural context, the origins of which are human life, human relationships, nature, life and death. The objective of this exhibition is to show how artists considered the events of the period and then created great paintings that tell us today how people preserved their humanity in such trying times.

Nikolai Romadin, an important socialist realist landscape painter, wrote the following: "Freedom is what all art is based on–freedom, unlimited freedom that catches the movements of the inner world."

Our exhibition is not a story of style and various artistic trends, but rather it is about the paintings themselves. They are the only true reality of art, and this is the basis on which we make judgements about art.

Russian artists of the Soviet era worked a lot for themselves, and not only for the state. Today it is the superior artistic quality of these works that impress us first. Secondly, despite one widely held opinion, the artists had not broken with pre-revolutionary artistic ethics, but continued to develop what had been created by previous generations.

The variety of artistic styles of the 20th century is strongly characteristic of modernism, which was undoubtedly based on artistic tradition. It was this enduring tradition that, together with personal talent of course, gave the totalitarian epoch's artists an opportunity to create true masterpieces.

It was figurative art that became the major repository of the traditions of two previous centuries. We see it not as blind repetition, but as a reflection of the past. In this artistic approach, renderings from life, as well as the avant-garde tradition, do not contradict realism. Such an approach to realism is characteristic of all artistic trends of the 20th century.

Russian art in general, as well as "socialist realism," were given an extra impetus by neoclassical tendencies characteristic of world art in the 1920s and 1930s and in particular within the cultural contexts of totalitarian regimes which treated tradition as a means to political ends.

It happened due to numerous negative social and political issues, such as the turmoil of wars and revolutions and also, undoubtedly, because of the crisis of the avant-garde and weariness of its abundant intelligence.

Mikhail LARIONOV. **Apple Tree after Rain.** 1906. Detail
Oil on canvas on board. 27⅜ x 27 in. (69,6 x 69,2 cm)

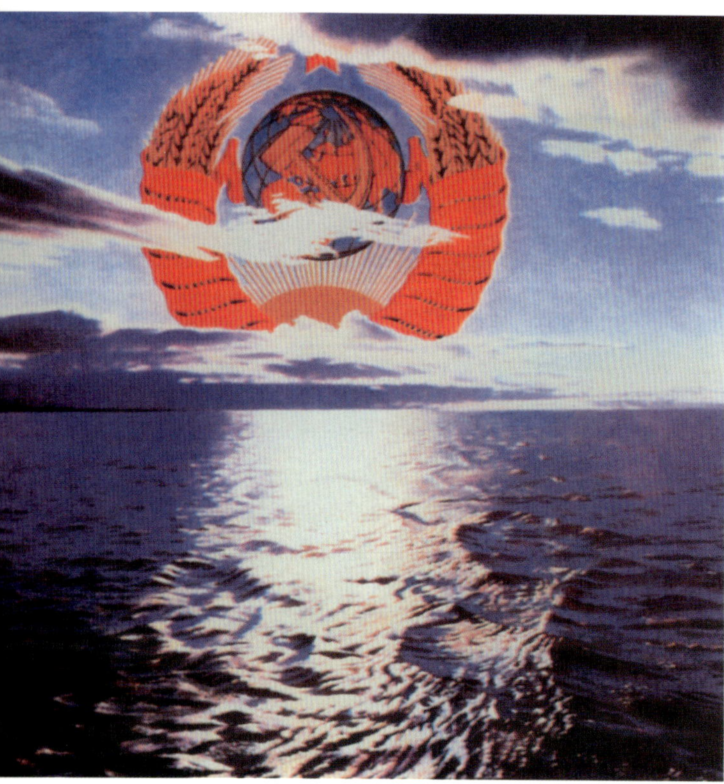

Erik BULATOV. **Sunset.** 1989. Oil on canvas. 78 x 78 in. (200 x 200 cm)

Picasso, Malevich, Derain, Moris de Vlaminck, Kuprin, Konchalovski, the artists of the Russian avant-garde and many others turned to the traditions of realism. A longing for stability and harmony made the artists turn to the "good old days" and start an intellectual play with the past. It is evident that every artistic trend interpreted the past in a different way. Generally speaking, playing with a subject from an earlier age became an essential feature of 20th century art throughout the world. Leonardo da Vinci was a particularly good example: Kazimir Malevich made a sticker saying "Apartments for Sale" and placed it in on a reproduction of *Mona Lisa.* The work became a part of the composition *Partial Eclipse* (1914). In 1923 Marcel Duchamp added a moustache to another reproduction of the famous painting. Fernand Leger produced a painting of Mona Lisa with keys in 1925, and finally, the celebrated Andy Warhol's image of Mona in his silkscreen series became famous.

Socialist realism also resulted from an intellectual play of the "world re-builders," and it was as irreconcilable as avant-garde. Its objective was to communicate with clarity to the masses and with subordination to the regime. And so it happened that Russian art based on the achievements of impressionism, Cezannism and critical realism of the 19th century resulted in the Moscow school of painting that had already been established. The school, along with avant-garde traditions, served as a basis for the art of the Soviet period.

Socialist Realism couldn't ignore it, even though the political dictate struggled against it: historically developed schools of teaching in Moscow and Leningrad functioned in their classical variants. This presupposed that mastery was passed from hand to hand: Valentin Serov and Igor Grabar were students of Ilya Repin; Aleksandr and Sergei Gerasimov were students of Valentin Serov; brothers Aleksei and Sergei Tkachev were students of Sergei Gerasimov; Boris Ugarov was a student of Igor Grabar and Aleksandr Gerasimov; and Ivan Sorokin was a student of Sergei Gerasimov. Socialist realism couldn't put into practice its principles of denying history and constructing totally new state and art systems–it was the point that made it similar to avant-garde. To deny the role of tradition in the life of art turned out to be impossible.

At the same time, throughout the whole world a return to the traditions of realism resulted in what is called neoclassicism, confirming the fact that art in the 20th century was developing similarly everywhere.

Moris Deni, who invented the notion of "neo classicism," proclaimed in 1924 at his birthday party: "Let's all return to the old order of Colbaire." Among those willingly turning to the "old" art was Pablo Picasso, who was reported by George Braque to have formerly "drunk gasoline to spew fire," particularly in 1914. He continued to improvise on the themes of Velasquez and Manet until the end of his life. Apollinaire told Picasso in 1918: "I want to see you making canvases as large as Pussen's". In the world context, a return to traditional values allowed artists to find "holes" that helped them shape their own style and individuality. This relates not only to Soviet art, whose representatives undoubtedly tried to avoid the political dictates of the state, but for the Western avant- garde artists as well. Quotations and stylization, along with an interpretation of styles from the past, broadened artistic opportunities.

Tradition in the 20th century and art in general is, on the one hand, a quintessence of everything that came before, and on the other, an impetus to its further development. Even avant-garde, which denied all traditions, finally became a tradition itself. It is particularly clear from the "idea of establishing an avant-garde museum" where the public would become well acquainted with the new art. In the end, avant-garde failed to achieve the goal its representatives had always purported: to leave the field of activities limited to museums and exhibitions.

This exhibition starts with two names, Ilya Repin and Valentin Serov, monuments of Russian art who greatly influenced all Russian art of the 20th century. And the fact that they taught many recognized Russian artists is not the only reason. The other reason lies in their own art. Repin's *Portrait of V.V. Stasov,* made in

1878, and a portrait of a Belgian pianist, Louise Merci D'Arjanto, made in 1890, are true masterpieces of realist portrait art that concentrated on the phenomenon of human personality.

The name of Valentin Serov (see his portrait *Mika Morozov*, made in 1901) is strongly associated with the introduction of one of the main principles of 20th century art. The establishment of lyricism in works of art shortened narration, thus shifting attention to the pictorial surface itself. Art was moving away from the plot and this defined the whole history of 20th century art. Russian art was heavily influenced by Impressionism and particularly by the figure of Paul Cezanne. The world context of fine art was not lost on Russia. The socialist realist artists, in spite of political bans, were guided by the principles of the Moscow school, admiring the discoveries of French impressionists and post-impressionists.

The value of a pictorial surface and the ability to play upon it, lightening the color palette, color shading, decorativeness, impasto brushstrokes, the abundance of plein air painting, and more – all these elements were cultivated and passed from teachers to students. As we have already mentioned, Igor Grabar is represented in this exhibition with his painting, *Snow in March* (1904). Grabar, one of the first advocates of impressionism in his early works, taught many Soviet artists.

An accent on the joyful, the establishment of decorative beauty in painting, color shading, the triumph of color – all these features became essential for socialist realist artists. It was particularly noticeable in works that they painted for themselves, rather than those commissioned by the government. *Trees in Bloom* by Aleksandr Gerasimov, *Still Life* by Yuri Katts, *Evening* by Sergei Gerasimov are examples of the highest mastery and painting technique.

The members of the avant-garde group, Jack of Diamonds, are represented with a later work by Petr Konchalovski *Floor-Polisher* (1946), *Still Life With Green Bottle* (1921) by Vasili Rozhdestvenski and *Self Portrait* (1923) by Robert Falk. All of these paintings were based on discoveries made by the impressionists, Cezanne and the post-impressionists, and these techniques were formulated into the artists' manifestos.

While in their early works they were enthusiastic about post-impressionism, later they, as well as the avant-garde in general, were heavily influenced by primitive folk art–see *Prostitute at the Hairdresser's* by Larionov (1914) and a futurist work by Lentulov, *Tower Gate. New Jerusalem* (1917), in which the idea of music is the painting's main concept.

The following works reflect the principles of the Moscow school of painting in the early 20th century: *Trees in Bloom* by Aleksandr Gerasimov (1930s), *Nude Masha* by Vasili Nechitailo (1976), *Novgorod. Yaroslav Monastery* by Vladimir Stozharov (1972), *Plesheevo Lake (August, Simak)* by Ivan Sorokin (1960), and *Post Girl in Winter* by brothers Aleksei and Sergei Tkachev (1951). They are not repetitious, rather each one of them is an individual work of art portrayed through the frame of a different epoch.

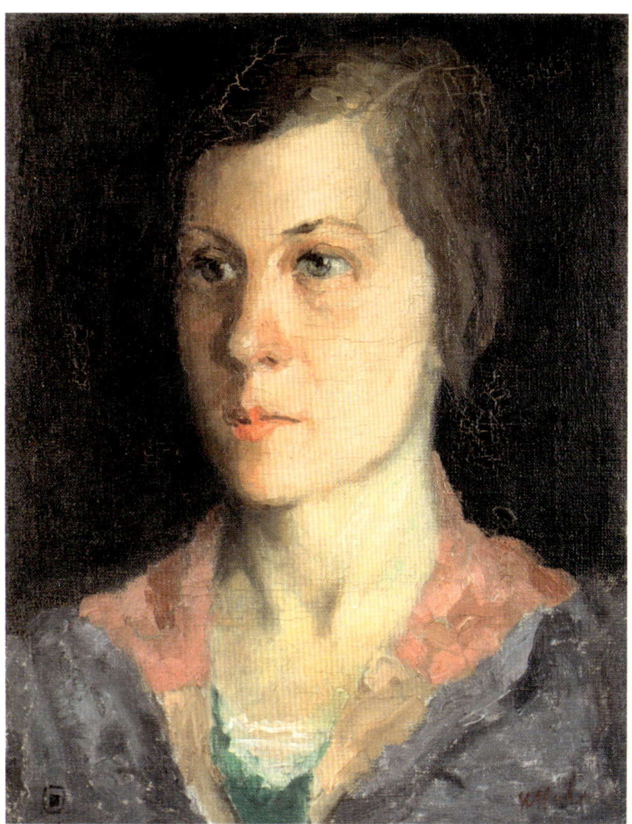

Kazimir MALEVICH. **Portrait of the Artist's Wife.** Early 1930s
Oil on canvas. 13¾ x 10⅝ in. (35,3 x 27,3 cm)

The way in which Russian art was developing is different from the way in which it developed in Europe, because in Russia all styles were emerging almost at one and the same time, rather than consecutively, as it happened in the West. That is why one can see manifestations of various styles in short artistic periods by one and the same artist.

To illustrate this point, one can refer to Filipp Malyavin, a student of Repin who initially was an icon painter, combining in his work, *Village Girl* (1903), expressionism and a decorative element of modernism. Though a viewer can see here no space depth, the booming colors and expression of movement take one into a sort of theatrical action. To compare: Baskakov in his *Milkmaids* (1962) seeks to achieve the same effect. Both pictures depict expressive emotions. The decorative pictorial origins and the compositional structure of the painting, with its low horizon, serve as the basic means of expression. But at the same time the

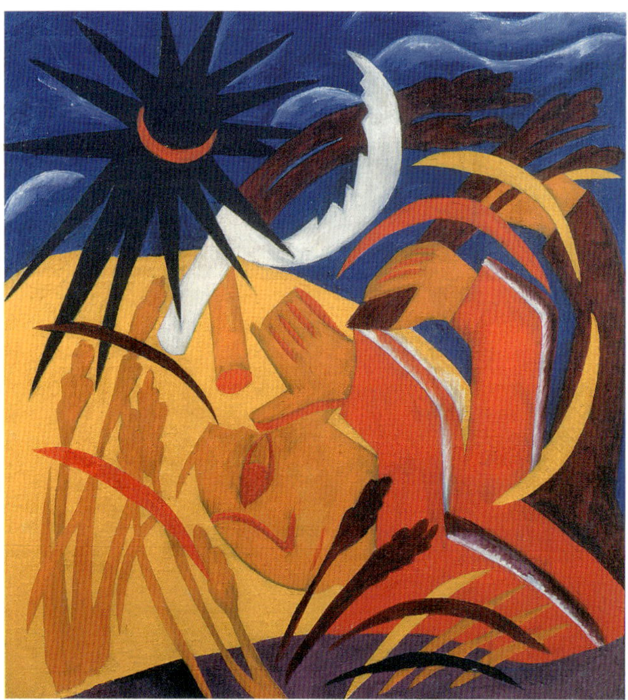

Natalia GONCHAROVA. **Harvesting.** 1911. Oil on canvas. 35⅞ x 38⅝ in. (92 x 99 cm)

ideological elements are absolutely different, which results in their difference in terms of artistic styles.

One of Petrov-Vodkin's most powerful masterpieces, *The Bathing of the Red Horse* (1912), has become accessible to the general public relatively recently. The communist ideology immediately filled it with revolutionary romanticism, though this painting still remains a mystery. Iconic-like decorativeness, along with powerful symbolist content, allows broad interpretation. This enigmatic work influenced a large number of Russian artists.

To observe the influence in the context of Soviet painting, one of its brightest manifestations can be seen in what is called the "Severe Style"–Soviet paintings of the 1960s and 1970s. Examples in this exhibition are *Remembering. Widows* and *Family in July* by Victor Popkov (1969), *Logging on the Vetluga River* by Eduard Bragovski (1964), *Aidan* by Tair Salahov (1967) as well as *Young Family* by Dmitri Zhilinski (1980) and *Marusya* by Geli Korzhev (1983–1989).

All these works demonstrate the strong individuality of the artists who painted them. Still, here we would point out a similar metaphoric character of the paintings, the many artistic languages of the context and a generality of images that are the means of expressing the artists' ideas.

Whether the plot is specific or general is no longer of importance to viewers. But paradoxically, it is still important to the artist himself. It is a well-known fact that the boy sitting on Petrov-Vodkin's horse is his own student, S. Kalmykov. In speaking with Geli Korzhev, we learn that *Marusya* is also a portrait. And the tarpaulin boots that symbolize in Russia the Soviet reality and the difficult lives of women is nothing more than a memory from the artist's life in communal apartments. Twelve families lived all together, sharing a single kitchen. Everyone wore tarpaulin boots because of the numerous rats that lived in the neighborhood.

An approach to the general from the specific thus elevates the sense of each painting to a level of signs and symbols. The decorative elements of the works' artistic language are similar due to an interest in line and the judicious concentration of intense color.

Within this essay we are perhaps unable to judge the role and place of tradition in the art of socialist realism. But we would note that "traditionalism" is one of the many "isms" in the art of this period, seen in its stylization and its allusions to recognized works from an earlier time. This fact makes it similar to the global artistic context. For historical reasons socialist realism was one of the longest lasting trends in 20th century Russian art and was hardly less radical than the Russian avant-garde. Its influence on Russian art that followed, i.e., contemporary art, is incredible.

The art of socialist realism wasn't static. It developed within itself, responding to political issues in the country. This exhibition strives to demonstrate this evolution by showing works made in various decades. For example, the 1930s saw the beginning of what came to be known as romantic socialist realism, as evidenced in works by Aleksandr Deineka, Georgi Nisski, Yuri Pimenov and others.

The 1940s and 1950s–the years of the "communist paradise"–are illustrated not by official painters (except Boris Yakovlev's *Soviet Canned Food* that was made intentionally for "The Industry of Socialism" exhibition), but by those who painted for themselves. One can see *Still Life* by Katts, *Evening* by Sergei Gerasimov, *Trees in Bloom* by Aleksandr Gerasimov, *Portrait of a Boy* by Gavril Gorelov, and *A Fresh Day* by Vladimir Gavrilov. In their efforts to avoid the pressure of the Communist Party, the artists often turned to unpopular genres that are somehow peripheral because of their scant political potential, such as landscapes, child portraits, etc. Many artists worked in these so-called "small" genres until the 1980s. The artists' paintings that illustrate this point are the Tkachevs' *Post Girl in Winter*, depicting their niece; Stozharov's *Novgorod. Yaroslav Monastery*, and Nechitailo's *Nude Masha*. Nechitailo portrayed his wife almost with an excursus to the painting of Renoir, on the one hand, and Rembrandt on the other.

The 1960s and the 1970s was a time of the post-Stalin Thaw when the value of human personality and the role of man as a creator of history became the major subject matters. The artists of that period were particularly influenced by the victory over fascism and human suffering and the end of the Stalin dictatorship. The times gave rise to the "Severe Style," probably named to counter Stalin's imposed "joyful style." The Severe Style artists featured in this exhibition are Viktor Popkov, Eduard Bragovski and Tair Salakhov.

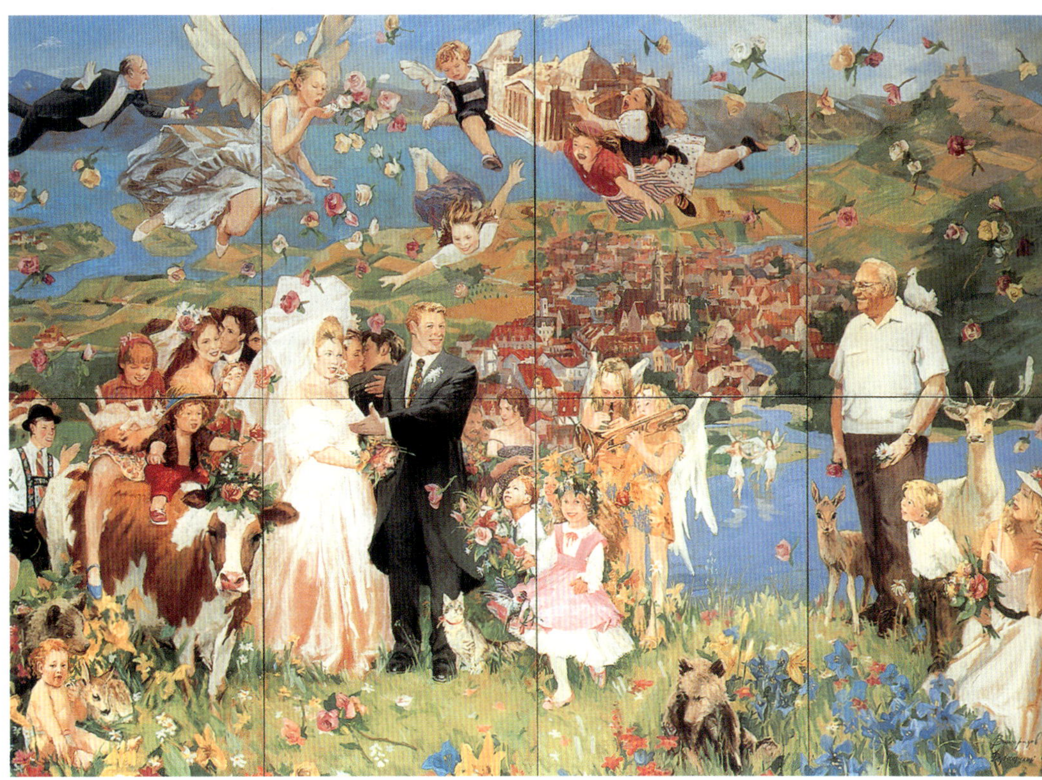

Aleksandr VINOGRADOV, Vladimir DUBOSSARSKY. **A Happy Day.** 1995. Oil on canvas. 156 x 312 in. (400 x 800 cm)

Igor Popov's *Our Yard* is characteristic of the 1970s. It is a philosophical reflection of the many aspects of human life. The simple yard of a Moscow apartment building is the setting that allows us to see the biblical progression of life: from childhood, love and family life to human death. The composition is organized according to the principle of a woven carpet, where the design has neither a beginning nor an end. While this intricate composition is decorative, it is much more than that: it succeeds in underlining the natural character of everything that happens in life, without drama and tension, but as an objective opinion. This philosophical understanding of life as a natural phenomenon independent from any outside influence, political or otherwise, makes this painting similar to a symbolic Russian icon and pre-Raphaelite painting.

The vision of an artwork as a symbol of an idea, even the simplest concept, unites all artistic trends of the 20th century, including socialist realism. The ideas themselves can be different: from ideologies to various avant-garde manifestos. Such a vision of allegory as a means of artistic expression became an essential feature of Russian art in the 1980s. Some examples are the works of Geli Korzhev (*Marusya*), Dmitri Zhilinski (*Young Family*) and Mai Dantsig (*Unmade Bed*).

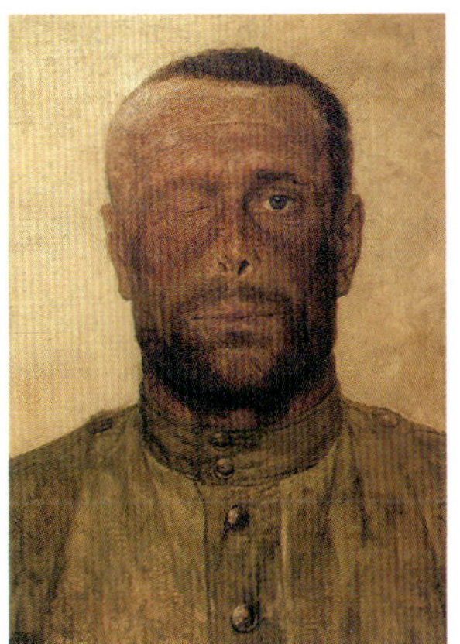

Geli KORZHEV. **A Soldier. Series: "Scorched by the Fire of War".** 1957–1960
Oil on canvas. 78 x 58½ in. (200 x 150 cm)

The influence of the art of the Soviet period is enormous, and by now it, too, has become a tradition. For example, the founders of Soc-art (V. Komar, A. Melamid and I. Kabakov), in their installations, and even Andy Warhol, who made several portraits of Mao as well as depictions of a hammer and sickle, continued to use socialist realism as "quotations" and symbols. Along with many other artists, they used its language in their intellectual games. A well-known art critic, V. Turchin, described the situation. Having in mind the artists of the next generations, he said: "They were Romans making copies from Greek originals, and they were pleased with them."

History always repeats itself. Such a trend during the last years of contemporary art will be understandable. A desire to paint and the motto of trans-avant-garde "To turn to the side of history!" and a tendency to understand painting as a tradition of making paintings, and many other things will bear witness to the fact that the law of negating negations is eternal. The history of art, as time passes and it finds itself far from this or that historical epoch, becomes wiser and more objective, realizing this simple truth: that however hard political influences are, they will sooner or later disappear, and art, first of all, is fed with the idea of preserving humanity and the human soul. That is why, whatever disasters can be told about political engagement, works of art themselves are always far more important, and they witness for themselves.

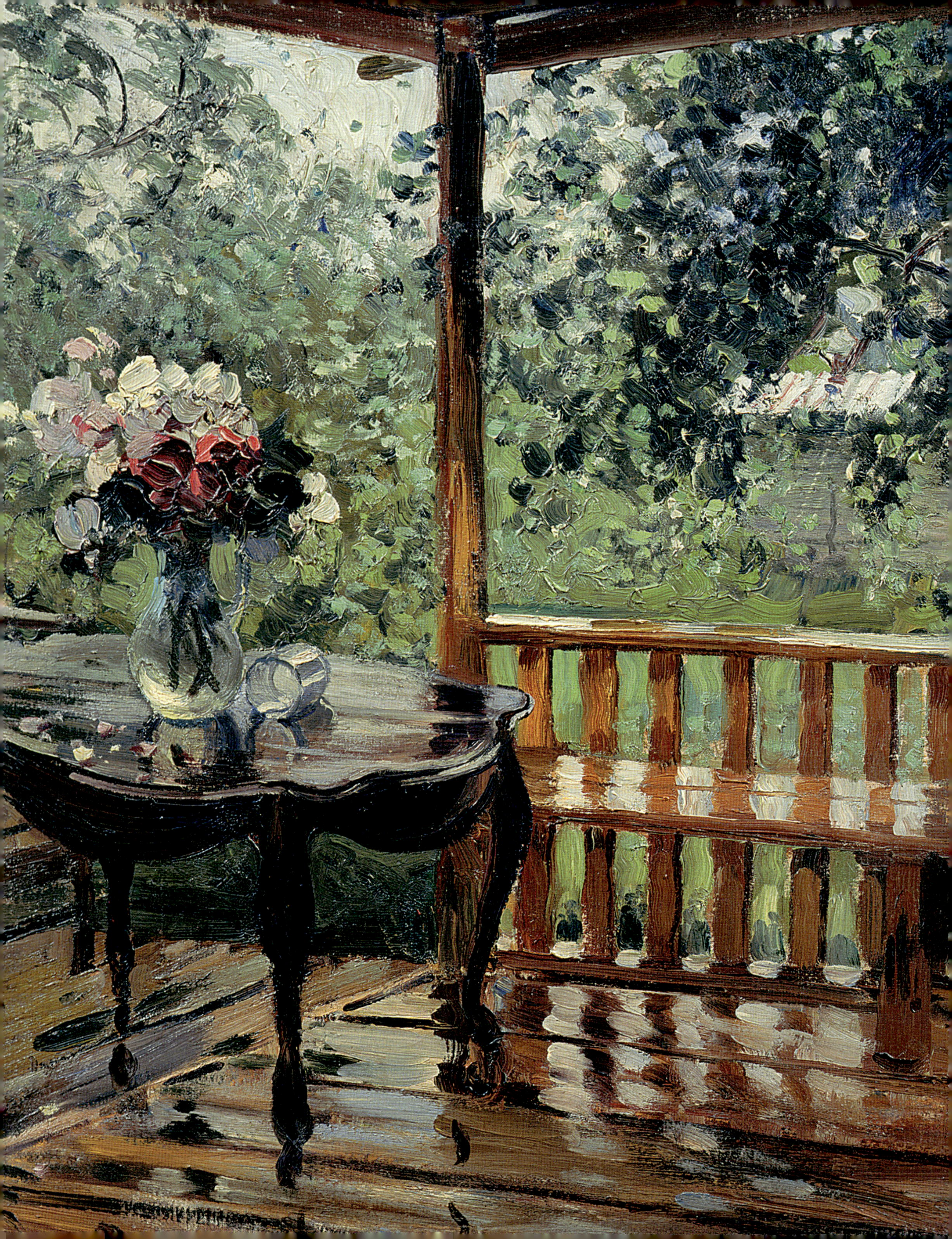

Tradition: The Gold Standard

Mikhail German

"Isn't to delete and erase from one's memory the shortest way to ignorance?"

Michelle de Montaigne

Self-aggrandizement as well as self-reproach is known never to be limited to any specific historic period. Alas, a historian can hardly be free from such a feeling. The issue is especially true for Russia, where self-knowledge has always been a painful process.

"It's only Russians, who now...have learned to be Russians to the greatest extent only when they have become Europeans to the same extent. And more than anything else, this distinguishes us from all other nations."[1]

Any art exists in a context, and the question is asked this way: to what extent is it recognized? It was only in the early years of the 20th century when Russian art began to be recognized with some respect in Europe, that at last an interaction of cultures began. Russian fine art, from Paris Seasons organized by Diagilev to the powerful experiments of Kandinsky, Goncharova and Larionov, Lentulov, El Lissizky and Malevich were recognized, establishing a stable position in the multinational iconographical sphere.

In Soviet times, even those artists who were far from receiving full official recognition (such as Pavel Kuznetsov) used to make trips to the West. But when the Iron Curtain fell, it was not long before artistic life in the Soviet Union was hermetically sealed from the rest of the world. As a result, a strong historical feeling of its "separateness"–and soon a feeling of inferiority – followed.

And this feeling is largely justified. Still, the art itself demands that scholars, from the distance of the ensuing decades, take a longer view.

A full hermetical separation can take place even in a culture where empowered officials exert no pressure, if the culture itself demonstrates indifference. Violence intensifies resistance as well as strong, though suppressed, inquisitiveness. Russian art of this era enjoyed a fruitful, though brief, historical period when Russian artists integrated into the European context and were influenced by impressionists such as Cezanne, Picasso and early expressionists. In Russia itself the Jack of Diamonds group, primitivism and abstraction emerged. Even years later, in formal structures such as the official OST, one notices traces of ideas that had been expressed by Mondrian. The issues of impressionism were argued in the official press as late as the 1930s[2], to say nothing of the avant-garde, whose powerful echo has always resonated in the art world.

One can see mutual influences as well as common stages in the general development of Russian art. In the 1930s, Western critics placed abstraction on almost the same level as salon art, and social commentaries were seen as artistic bravery. Due to this, the interest in fairly traditional socialist realism in the West was somewhat intensified. As for the USSR, the avant-garde (commonly believed in the West to be almost the only phenomenon in 20th century Russian art worthy of attention) preserved the traditions of innovation, and its suppression intensified its popularity in the West. The sinister mirror of official propaganda cast distorted reflections on these phenomena, but they existed and Deineka's works also existed and strangely resonated with those praised by Mussolini and Hitler.

Although the Russian avant-garde played a significant role in artistic development in the 20th century and socialist realism was dramatically installed, the two movements do not tell the entire story, any more than any nation's schools can be completely expressed by their radical movements.

Russian scholars cannot–and should not–allow the crystal of aesthetics to be the only prism through which to view the history of art. Excessive objectivity borders dangerously on moral conformity, and history demands than an art professional be incredibly accurate, knowl-

Aleksandr GERASIMOV. **After Rain.** 1935. Detail
Oil on canvas. 29¼ x 33⅛ in. (78 x 85 cm)

[1] F. Dostoeveski, Full Collection of Works, Leningrad, 1975, Vol. 13, p. 377

[2] "An artist who is a poet and a philosopher seeks to foretell our future on the basis of today and demonstrates it in his painting. But this already forces him to surpass the borders of fact and bring in fantasy and imagination. Do such violations of 'nature' correspond to the principles of socialist realism? Because one can thus become a symbolist. May the symbolism be? May the romanticism be?" N. Shekotov, Painting (At the exhibition "The Industry of Socialism"), Art Magazine, 1939, No. 4

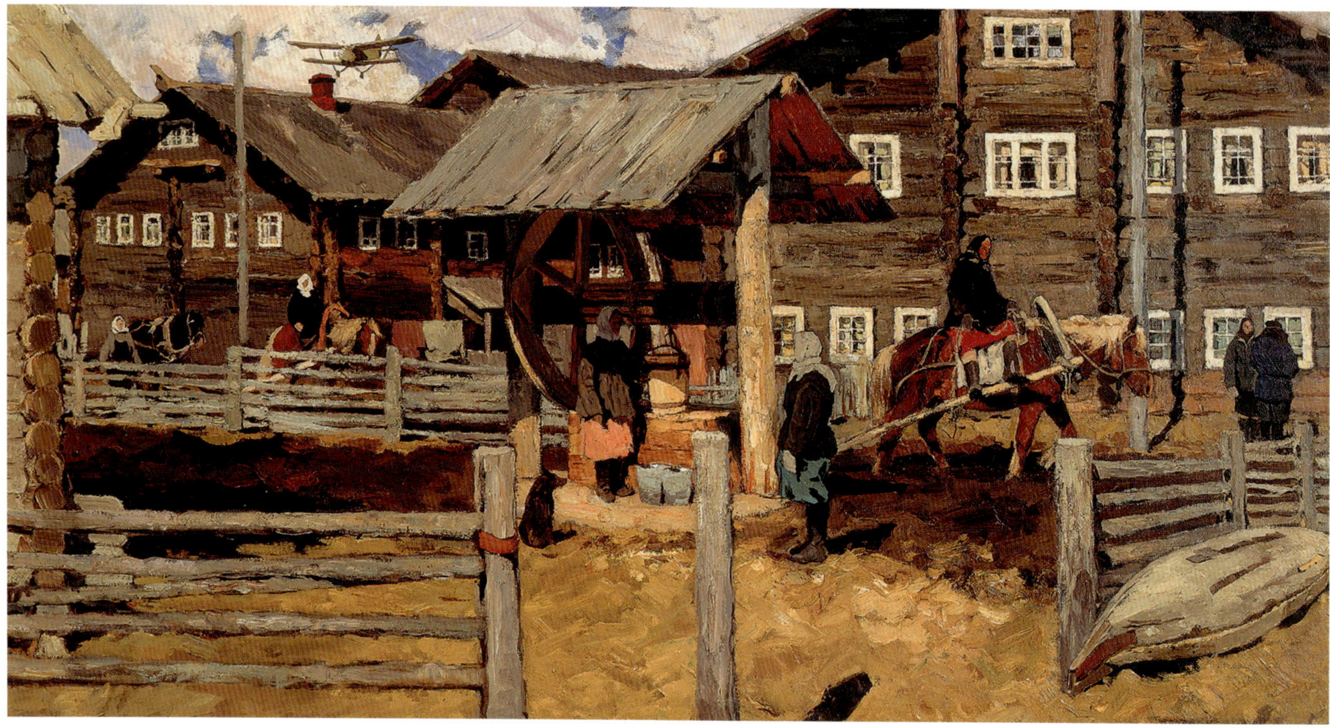

Vladimir STOZHAROV. **Well in the Carpathians.** 1962–1964. Oil on board. 38¼ x 72¼ in. (97 x 184 cm)

edgeable, and have balanced opinions and an uncompromising ethical memory. "Sine ira et studio" – without anger and partiality for–the expression holds the critic to a high standard.

A historic cliche is that the avant-garde was "stopped on the run" by the sovereign will and socialist realism triumphed. While this may appear correct on the surface, further thought leads to this alternative question: Imagine that the avant-garde had "won" and had occupied the position as the historic, official art. In Russia, this, too, would not have led to diversity; on the contrary, intolerance for socialist realist art would have led to a struggle for artistic freedom. The development of high modernism and post-modernism presupposes tolerance, and the irreconcilability of these artistic positions, the heavy political engagement, and the total lack of will to recognize the necessity of pluralism cancelled any possibility of the development of high modernism and post-modernism in Russia.

While this is unfortunate, even sadder is the great Malevich's intolerance for socialist realist art that bordered on Bolshevist fanaticism.

What has forced the integral image of 20th century Russian and Soviet art itself out of the focus of serious scholarship? In short, it has been the polarization of historic artistic positions. Now, with the passing of time have come more tolerance and some wisdom. We are simply not right to ignore some of the important well known and lesser known aspects of our culture. We must recognize the influence of our country's bloody and tragic history, remembering that Russian history before 1917 did not differ significantly with its history after the revolution, and recalling that all suffering was an overwhelming ingredient in our culture through decades of totalitarianism.

Here arises the critical and often forgotten, or neglected, issue of artistic quality.

In most 20th century art museums, the bombing of Guernica will become no more than an annotation to the great painting by Picasso. Although an extremely important historical event, the bombing itself will be remembered only as the subject of one of the world's art masterpieces. This is simply a reality that we are powerless to change.

But if the present generation will courageously see the art, without forgetting the blood and gloom, future historians will be able to avoid preconceptions or misconceptions, conscious or unconscious. Because, as it wisely said by Heidegger: "An epoch can never be cancelled by a disclaiming sentence." Indeed, we cannot afford to forget the painful periods in our history, but having realized our own voluntary dependence on it, we can preserve a measure of objectivity.

Twentieth-century Russian art, in its artistic essence, has always preserved those qualities, which allows us now to describe it simply as art.

And I am not referring to the underground avant-garde.

In the totalitarian era there were almost no underground artists. Most of the well known avant-garde masters were, in greater or lesser degrees, loyal to the official ideology, at least in their professional lives. Nearly all wanted to participate in the prestigious official exhibitions that received much publicity. Even Filonov painted a portrait of Stalin. And the boom of history deafened even those who were far more rationally minded than artists.

Here I do not mean the hidden opposition–it was small, but it still existed. I am referring to those paintings that were created just because the artists wished to paint, loved art itself as a profession, and put their own souls into their canvases–not for someone else, but for themselves.

The discerning viewer will notice at just a glance two commonalities that unite masters of the early 20th century with serious, though less famous, artists of the mid-century. All of them demonstrate a passion for figurative art, and all received good training.

The conservative methods of the old Academy of Arts (the official name was changed, but it continues to be called by its former name) had a profound effect on its students. There they were able to teach skills and techniques, and despite what the future held for each graduate, all maintained their professionalism. The words of a Chinese philosopher states that only one who masters the rules can successfully innovate. This expression is very important for today's graduates of Russian artistic institutions. Generally speaking, students producing abstract art or contemporary installations who have acquired academic basics create much better art than amateurs who burst into the artistic mainstream without the support of the "gold standard" of professional, traditional teaching.

As early as 100 years ago, Russian artists discovered variables that apply to creating figurative art. Ilya Repin, in his late 19th century portraits, managed to depict the fleeting psychological state of a subject and, at the same time, express air and light. He succeeded in portraying not so much the eyes, but rather the sight; not the face, but rather its expression. Some variable of the impressionistic vision thus acts as an integral part of a psychological character, capturing a moment in time. One is reminded of the words of Merezhkovski regarding symbolism: "The very style and artistic material of poetry become spiritual through symbolism."[3]

This quotation fits well into our context, as the symbolic basis in our poetry originated not from the theme, as it did with Von Stuck, but from the texture of art itself, as with Vrubel. The perfect artistry of Valentin Serov united the art of two ages without destroying or abolishing anything. Serov was the first to render the psychological as aesthetic and managed to do so delicately, even to a greater extent than did Repin.

In the period of pre-revolutionary culture, when there was no censorship, figurative art loomed large and

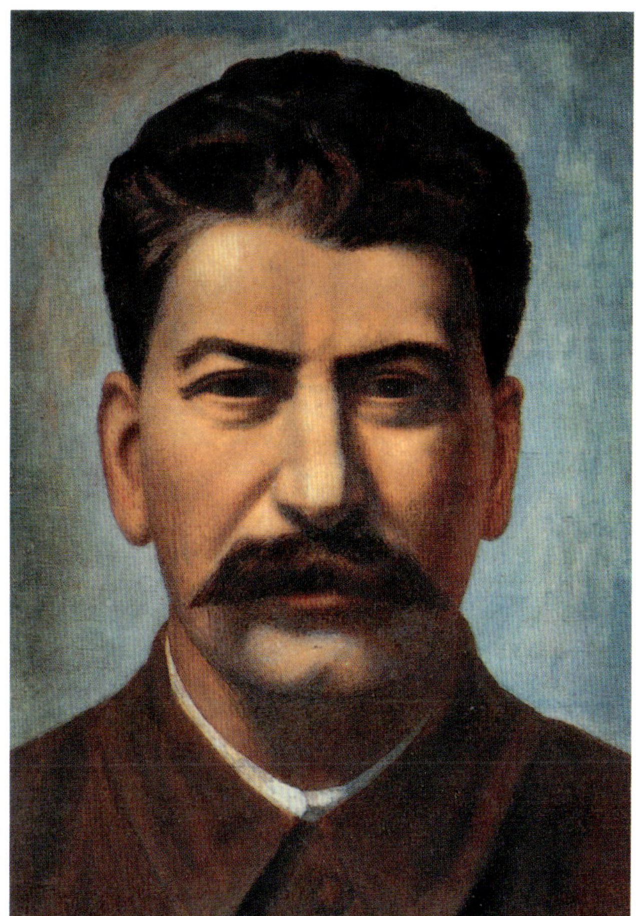

Pavel FILONOV. **Portrait of Stalin.** 1936
Oil on canvas. 38⅞ x 26⅛ in. (99 x 67 cm)

assumed importance. A famous work by Kuzma Petrov-Vodkin, *The Bathing of the Red Horse* (1912, The State Tretyakov Gallery), is both passionate and stunning. Other examples are the works of the icon, Zinaida Serebryakova, who painted with strict subtlety and sense of style; the breathtaking, colorful phantasmagorias of Filipp Malyavin; and the powerful primitivism of Mikhail Larionov. These examples point to a wide range of artistic rubrics united by traditional orientation toward subject and techniques, despite the broad differences in the artists' visions.

But in the early 1930s the state's interference in artistic life dictated that each piece of art reflect the socialist ideology. This dictum forced most professional artists to lead a double life, whether intentionally or unintentionally. Those talented masters who loved their art and were unlikely to fall under the spell of politics painted often for themselves. Every regime in every era sees artists who love to paint for their own fulfillment.

Today, socialist realism is seen only as the ghost of Bolshevik's ideology, and one can easily laugh at some-

[3] D. S. Merezhkovsky. Full Collection of Works, St. Petersburg, 1975, Vol. 13, p. 377

thing now known to be false. It is more difficult to delve into complex problems, realizing the process of voluntary vs. obligatory, and the difference between auto-suggestion and self-delusion without losing sight of the reasons for mass optimism at that time. "Unfortunately, the rush to judge finally cancels one's wish to explain,"[4] wrote the great historian, Mark Block, some 50 years ago. Analyzing cultural and historical issues in overcrowded political battlefields has always prevented the assessment of historical events, let alone the ability of anyone to predict them.

All those elements that were commonly named "French tradition," or in other words, the cult and aesthetics of extravagant color, refined technique and intentional indifference to the theme, could not be forgotten. Great examples of brilliant painting technique have been carefully preserved in Soviet museums and in the memory of elder generations. It was not only the art of those who, like Robert Falk, managed to spend so many years in Paris, or Petr Konchalovski, whose art matured with "Russian Cezannism". Even Petr Williams, who had no direct dialogue with the West, though painted with a truly European vividness and came close to Western themes, was part of the transnational artistic culture.

I want to repeat: there is influence and there are common, phased stages of development. From the time surrealism flourished in New York and Paris and the appearance of Marcel Duchamp's early works to the time *Breakfast in Furs* by M. Oppenheim had become nearly routine, Russian ("Soviet") art maintained the traditions of rendering figurative works, preserving the opportunities provided by state schools. Themes and styles that were "routine" in Western, lifelike art, from Hopper's severe photorealism to Alber Marquet's tough and tender asceticism, were to stay hidden in the Soviet Union. There, a work of art without an idea of or reference to socialist topics of the day could rarely if ever be exhibited, let alone be a success.

Despite the difficulties, art survived.

Even those artists who were treated kindly by the state and thus included in the official history of Russian art as creators of important paintings that praised the state, when left alone with their works remembered the contract they had with their art, their talent–half-strangled yet still alive. Even Vasili Efanov, who has always been viewed as part of the Stalin era's triumphal pompousness, demonstrates in one of his later works, a small sketch, *Marinka*, the artistry and temperament of a true master that overcame his shady reputation as a "court painter."

Art appears to protect artists, even those who were part of the official state culture, from full surrender, bringing them back to the time of true, artistic joy. Art itself contains the breath of freedom. Even in the worst years, people did not stop loving, being happy and bringing up children, because in every life there is a place for happiness as well as for sadness. And you can hardly find an artist who, for at least a day or an hour, has not felt himself simply an artist, a happy contributor to the profession.

"Human life becomes true suffering, a real hell, only when two eras, two religions, two cultures come together."[5] These words by Herman Hesse appeal to thinkers, perhaps mostly artists, who are prone to reflect on painful experiences or events. On the other hand, visual art that introduces the material delights of real life, in the process of becoming, restores an artist's balance.

The "Severe Style" that finalized Soviet art in the 1960s included both the early works of artists such as Yuri Pimenov, Georgi Nisski and Leonid Kabachek, and the newly discovered achievements of the new, still almost prohibited avant-garde.

In the period of the "thaw," that did not last long, art again pictured tragedy, the authentic suffering, war, grief and love that had nothing in common with pathos, sentimentality and triumph. The art of this period found a natural fulcrum in what Italian neo-realists call a "document taken to the level of poetry." Incidentally, the early paintings of Guttuso, Bernard Bofuet, as well as Italian and Polish movies, were embraced by the Russian "Severe Style" artists, who admired this brave and shockingly truthful art in cinematic form.

Among many artists of the period, both Geli Korzhev and Viktor Popkov excelled at building a unique artistic world of "small tragedies." Along with some of the best writers of their time, such as Trifonov and Astafiev, they constructed a material world of complicated metaphors populated with their human subjects, and proving again that there can be no art without a range of free will.

Time changes many things. Taste in one era gives way to a different taste in another time. But how can one deny that in the area of high modernism (post-modernism is still too unclear as a phenomenon among myriad quick interpretations) there can be no place for preconceptions and intolerance? In art, only artistic quality is of real importance.

No one doubts the long standing opinion that dictators kill art. Still, another long held opinion regarding the immortality of art can hardly be revised either. Yet a researcher who does not seek out real answers after discovering flaws in earlier thinking is hardly worthy of respect.

---

[4] M. Block. Apology of History, Moscow, 1986, p. 80

[5] H. Hesse. Collection of Works, St. Petersburg, 1994, Vol. 2, p. 209

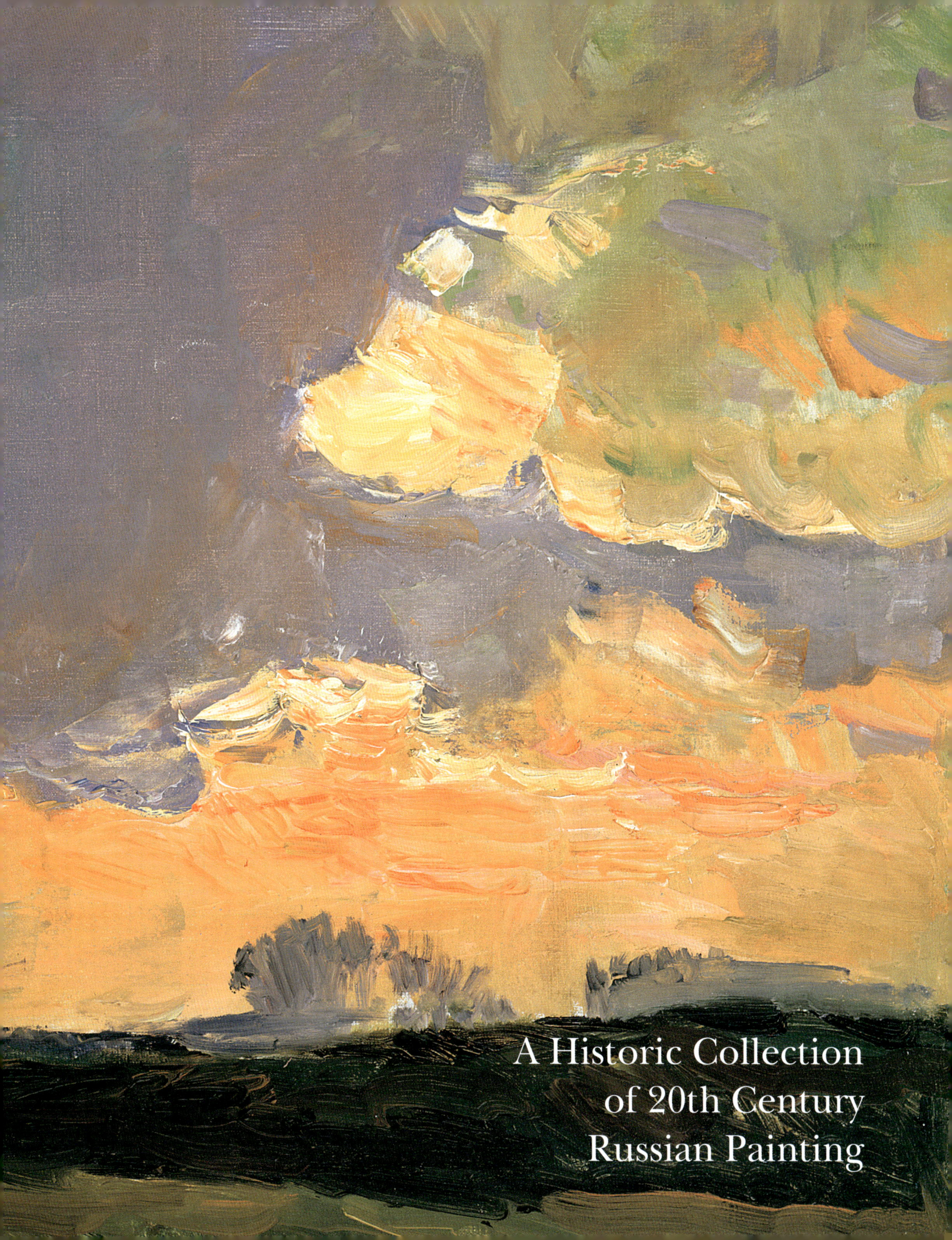
A Historic Collection
of 20th Century
Russian Painting

Ilya E. REPIN

1844 – 1930

Portrait of V.V. Stasov. 1873
Oil on canvas, 30½ x 24½ in.
(78 x 63 cm)
The State Tretyakov Gallery
Moscow, Russia

V.V. Stasov was an art and music critic, an architect with a passion for art, one of the ideologists of The Wanderers (Itinerants) and an influential man of arts in the second half of the 19th century. Stasov sat for Repin many times, but the artists loved this portrait most of all, believing that it "expresses this passionate youngster who is more than 50 years old." In his writing, Repin portrayed Stasov as "...a knight in the purest sense of the word. He seemed to be born for the arts...."

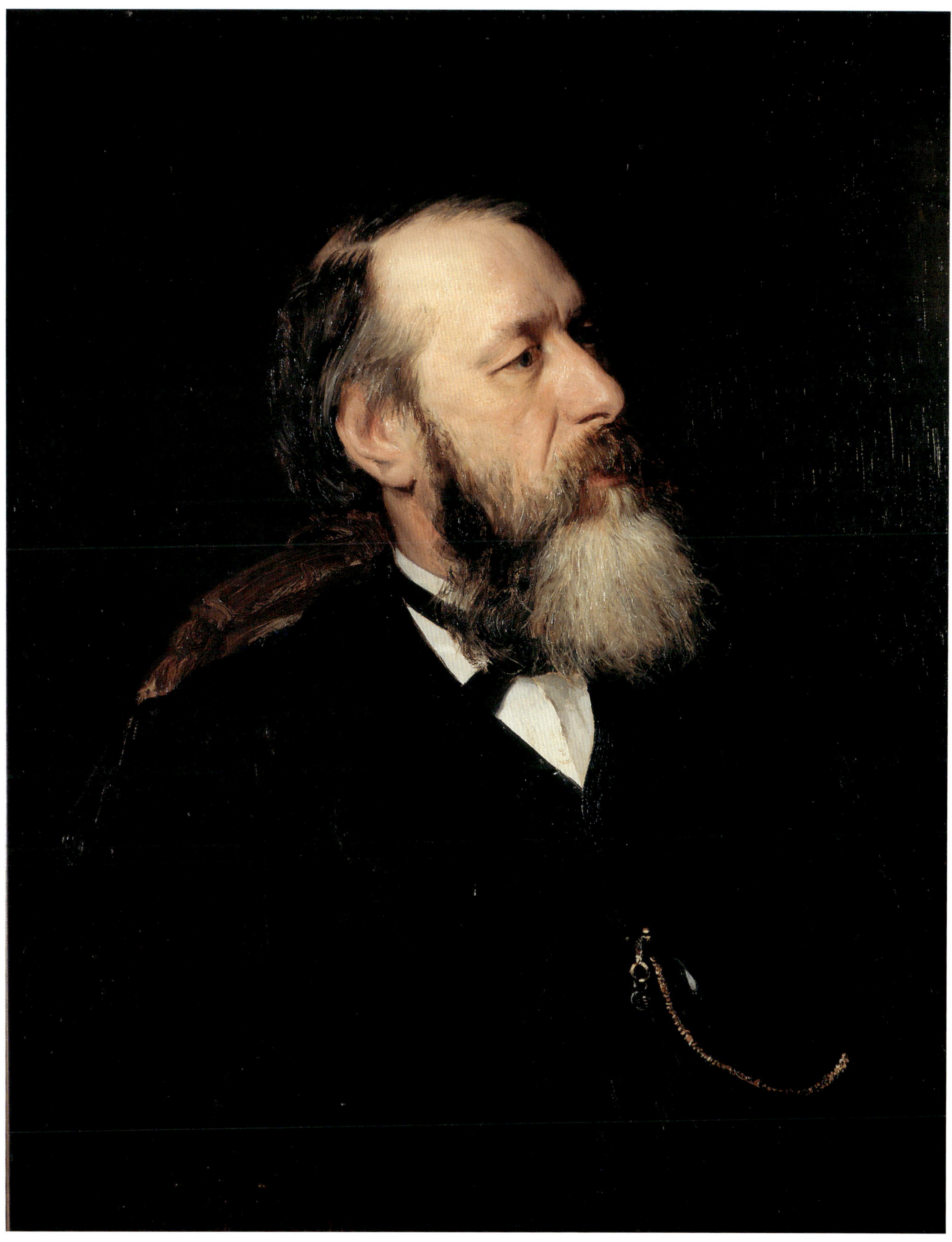

Ilya E. REPIN

1844 – 1930

Portrait of L. Merci d'Arjanto, a Pianist. 1890
Oil on canvas. 33⅜ x 42⅛ in.
(85,4 x 108 cm)
The State Tretyakov Gallery
Moscow, Russia

The artist depicted the Belgian pianist, Princess Carmont-Schime, who admired and advocated Russian music. Mrs. d'Arjanto loved Russia and spent her last years in St. Petersburg. Repin painted her portrait, commissioned by Ts. Kui, a well-known Russian composer, not long before she passed away.

Repin's outstanding works amazed viewers and other artists, as well. Grabar, Repin's pupil, remembered the master: "...It was quite remarkable and surprising to us that we couldn't ever paint anything equal to his art... It was inconceivable – we had some 20 paints in our palette, the best foreign paints available, but our results were dull, while he had only ochre, black, white and blue paints, some five or six colors, no more...and here you are, all his paintings are in full bloom, sparkling like pearls...."

(My Life, Moscow, 1937, p. 117)

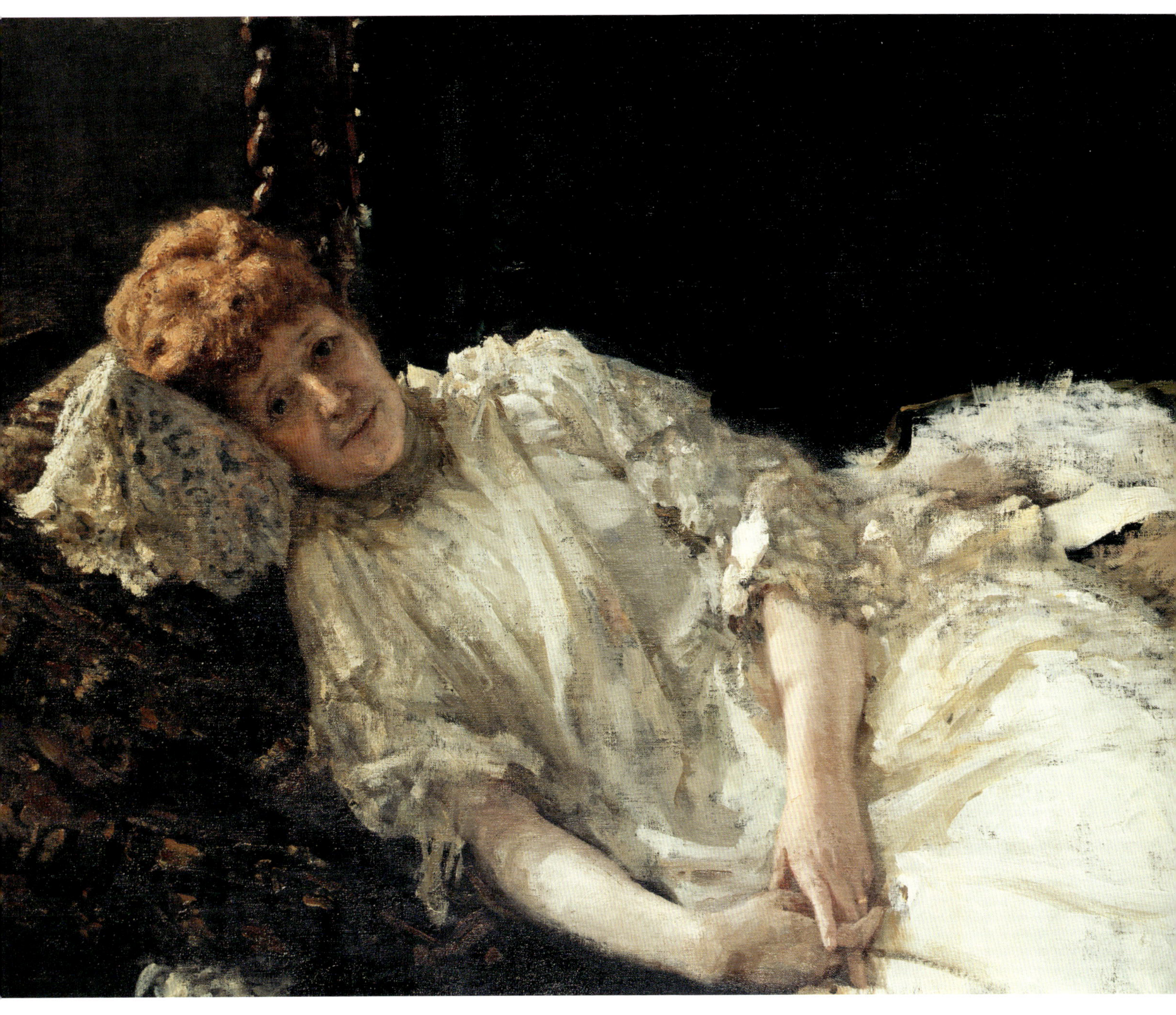

Valentin A. SEROV

1865 – 1911

Mika Morozov. 1901
Oil on canvas. 24¼ x 27½ in.
(62,3 x 70,6 cm)
The State Tretyakov Gallery
Moscow, Russia

Valentin Serov's paintings are veritable feasts of light and color. In the portrait of Mika Morozov, the son of art collector M.A. Morozov of the famous Morozov-Tversky dynasty, the artist created a harmonic image of a lively and emotional child. The boy, who later became a well-known philologist, Shakespeare expert, writer and playwright, has just seen something beyond the picture and seems to be ready to vanish from our sight.

"He (Serov) was a talented portraitist," noted the subject's mother, Margarita K. Morozova. "The portrait of my son, Mika, exhibited now in the Tretyakov Art Gallery, is particularly successful...."

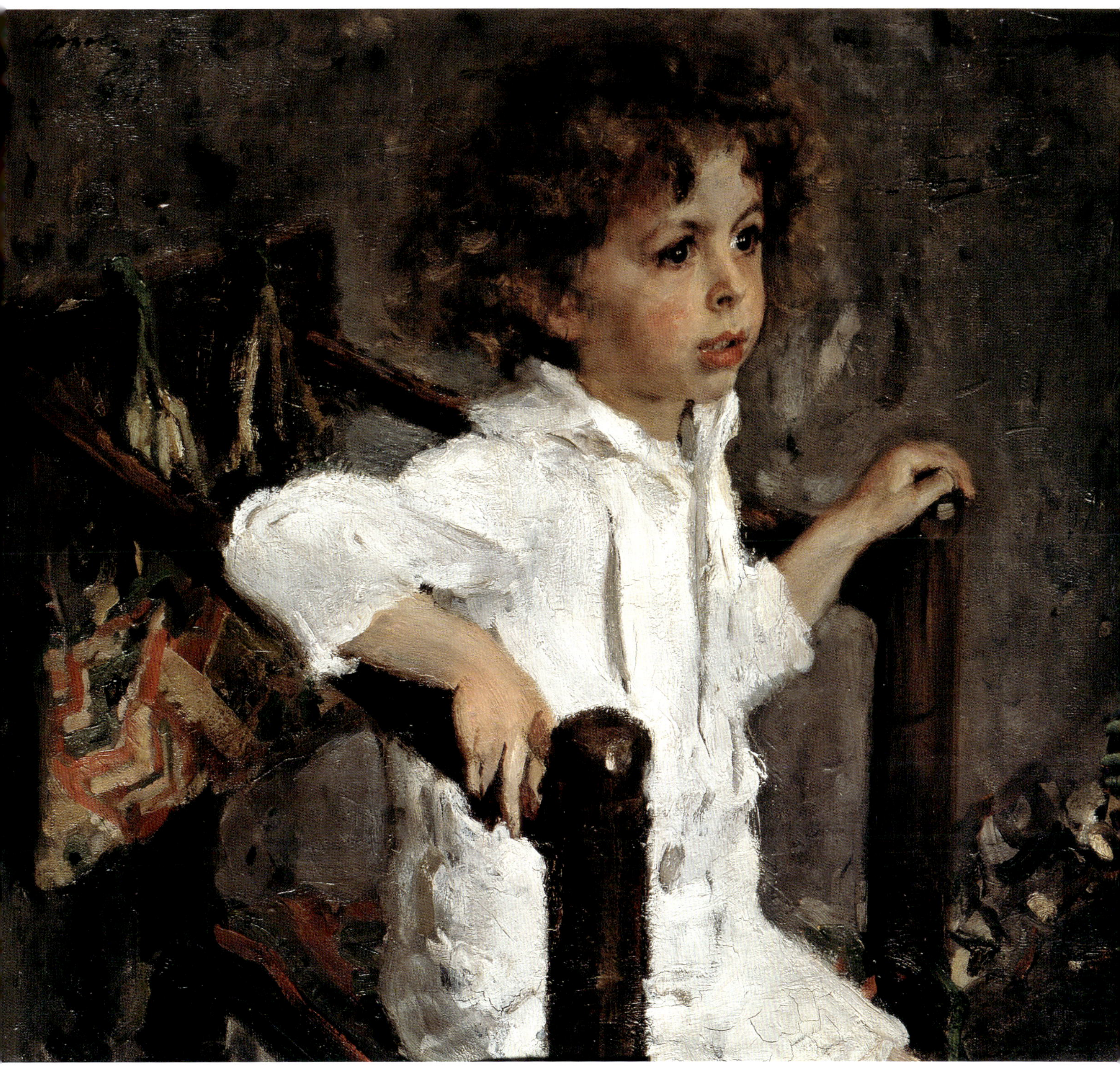

Filipp A. MALYAVIN

1869 – 1940

Village Girl. 1903
Oil on canvas. 80½ x 45 in.
(206,3 x 115,6 cm)
The State Tretyakov Gallery
Moscow, Russia

A student of Ilya Repin, Malyavin earned his fame as the creator of an entire gallery of Russian peasantry. His village women burst into Russian art at the beginning of the 20th century like a picturesque flood.

In the words of Igor Grabar, "His...village women are not just portraits and studies, but a whole unique world unknown before.... He (Malyavin) depicts their personalities, quite real and tangible, but also as ethereal creatures. He turns village girls and women into fantasy figures, sparkling with incredible colors...."

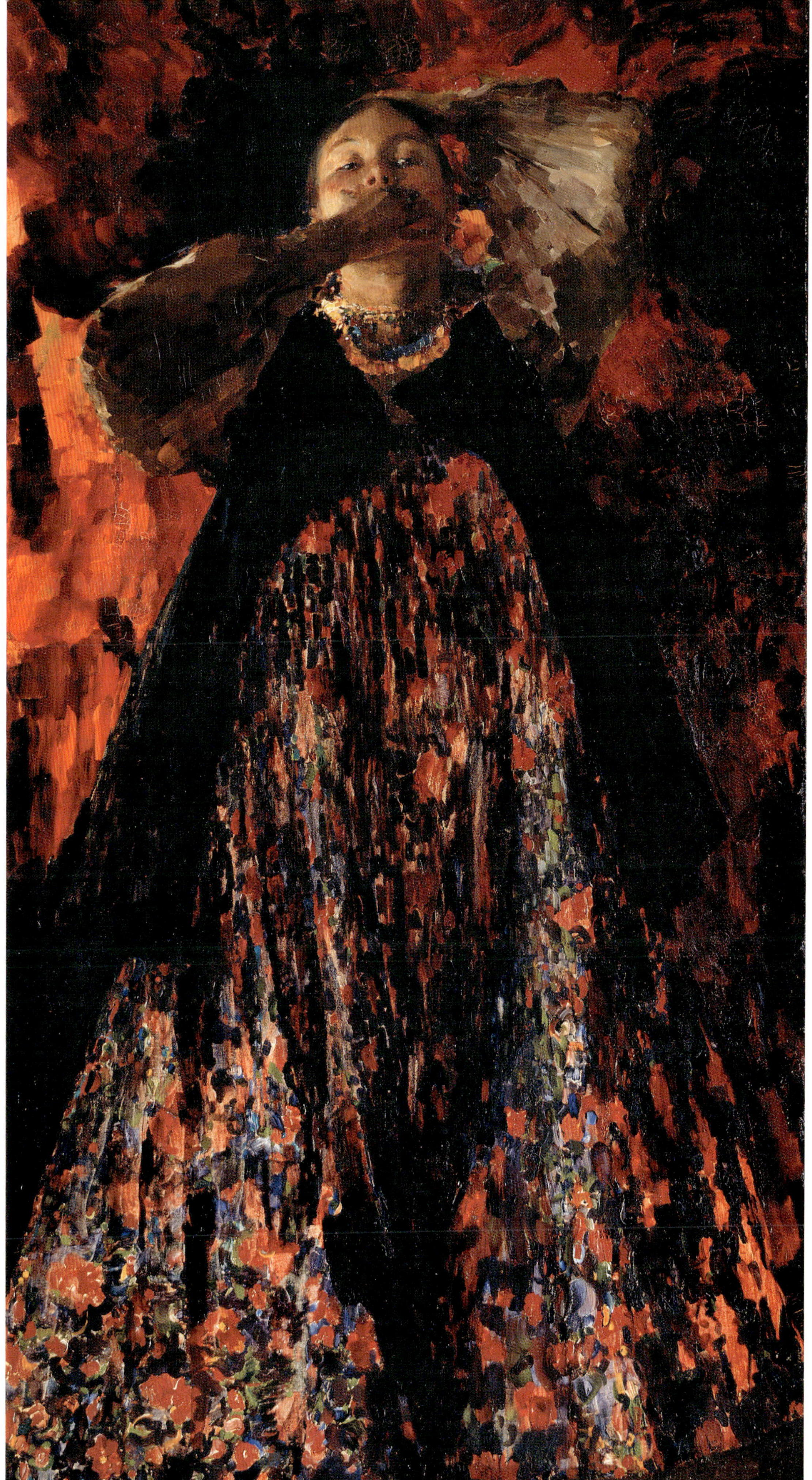

Igor E. GRABAR

1871 – 1960

Snow in March. 1904
Oil on canvas. 31¼ x 24½ in.
(80 x 63 cm)
The State Tretyakov Gallery
Moscow, Russia

An outstanding theoretician, Russian art historian, and one of the directors of the Tretyakov Gallery, Grabar received his art education in Munich, Paris, and in St. Petersburg at the Imperial Academy of Arts.

Snow in March was created not far from the Dugino manor. Grabar described this especially fulfilling time in his life as an artist. "During February, March and April I indulged myself, throwing myself into my work and painting from life from morning until night. I was overwhelmed by the wonders of nature-by snow falling in March, melting in the sun and showing tracks from horses and human footprints. On sunny days I saw symphonies of colors and shapes, and shadows cast on the snow under a blue-green tree. As I was about to finish the painting I noticed a village girl walking across the road with buckets hanging from her shoulders. I called out to her, asking her to stop for just 10 minutes while I painted her into the landscape. The whole study was completed in a single sitting. I painted with passion, throwing paints on the canvas in a frenzy... just trying to paint my impressions of that girl and the scene full of joie de vivre...."

(Automonograph, Moscow, Leningrad, 1937. p. 213)

Grabar's art greatly influenced many generations of Russian artists.

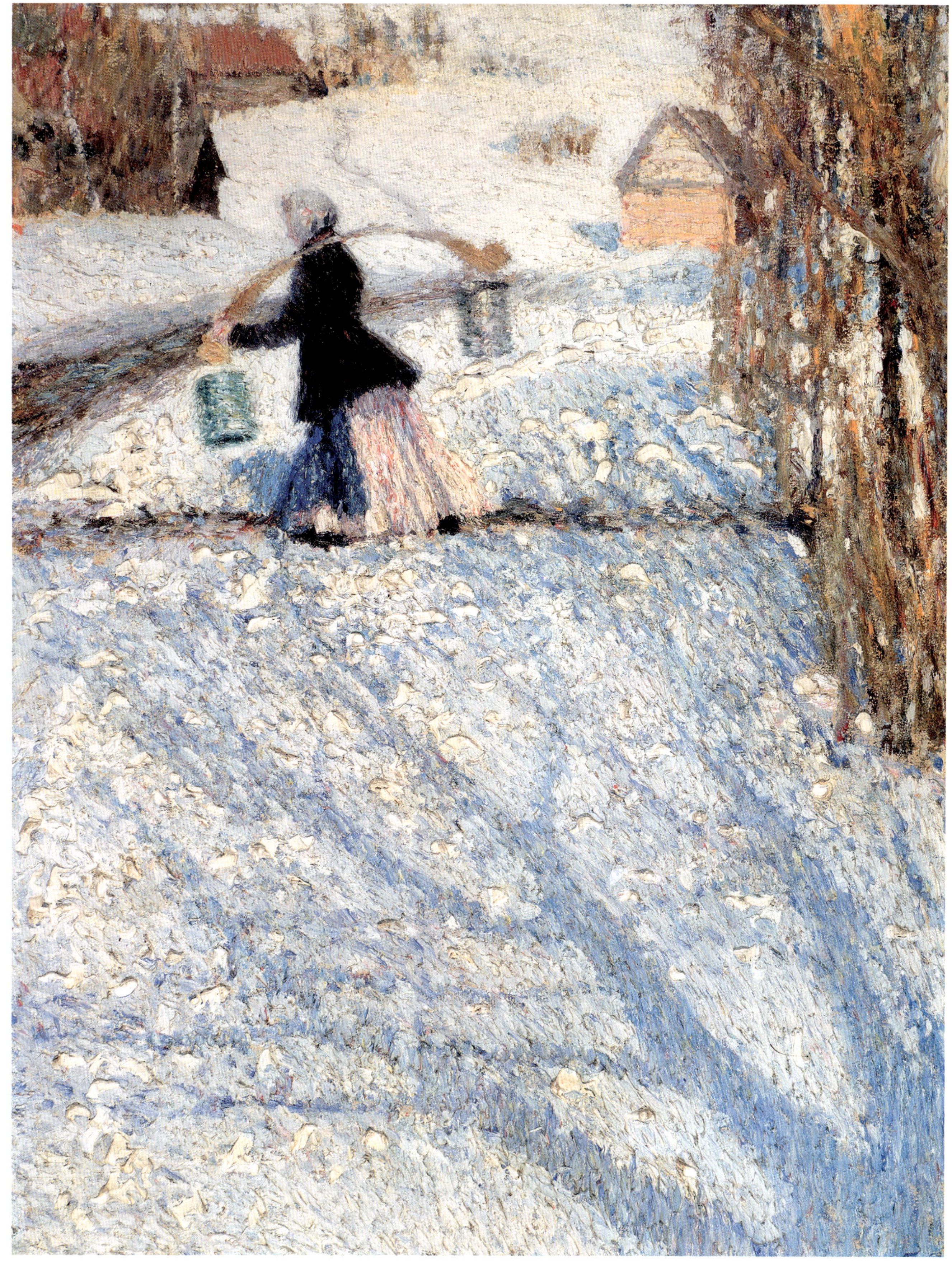

Nikolai I. FECHIN

1881 – 1955

Portrait of Artist's Wife. 1910s.
Oil on canvas. 26 x 29¼ in.
(65 x 73,5 cm)
From a Private American Collection
Loan arranged by
The Museum of Russian Art
Minneapolis, Minnesota USA

Portrait of Artist's Wife was preserved by Fechin's heirs for many years bearing disfiguring vertical stripes painted wide across the portrait. In the course of restoration it became clear that the artist disfigured the painting immediately after he finished it. It is thought that the painting reflects a family drama, Fechin's departure for the United States in 1922 and a quick divorce from his wife-model.

This masterpiece is exhibited publicly for the first time since its restoration.

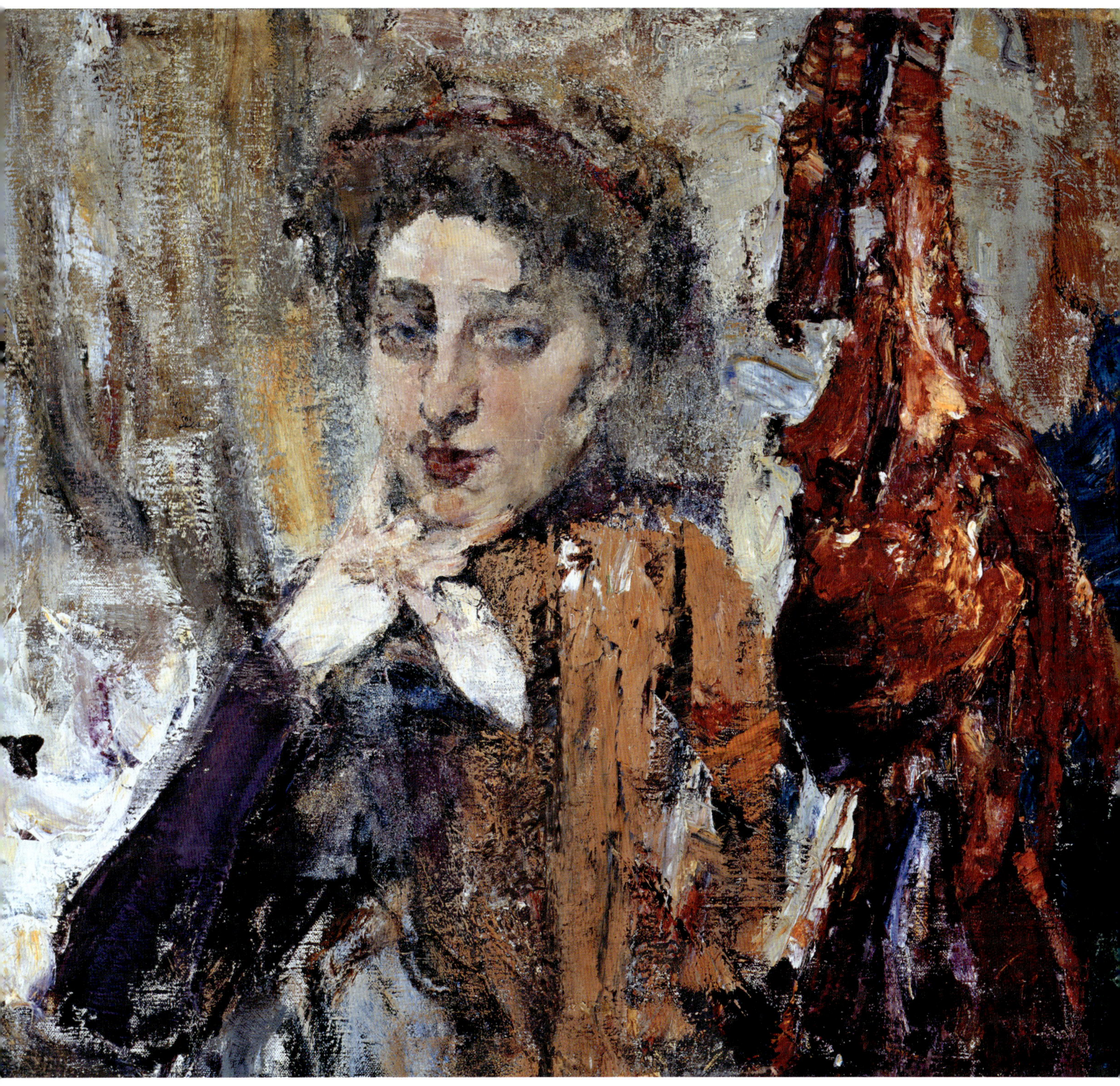

Kuzma S. PETROV-VODKIN

1878 – 1939

The Bathing of the Red Horse. 1912
Oil on canvas. 62½ x 72½ in.
(160 x 186 cm)
The State Tretyakov Gallery
Moscow, Russia

The Bathing of the Red Horse, Petrov Vodkin's most famous painting, had been acknowledged as a prophetical work long before the tragic events took place in the 20th century. The young boy with a fixed, direct gaze seems to hover on the red horse above the earth.

The artist combined in his art the ancient Russian icon painting technique, its rich spirit, symbolic color and the principles of the early Italian Renaissance monumental painters.

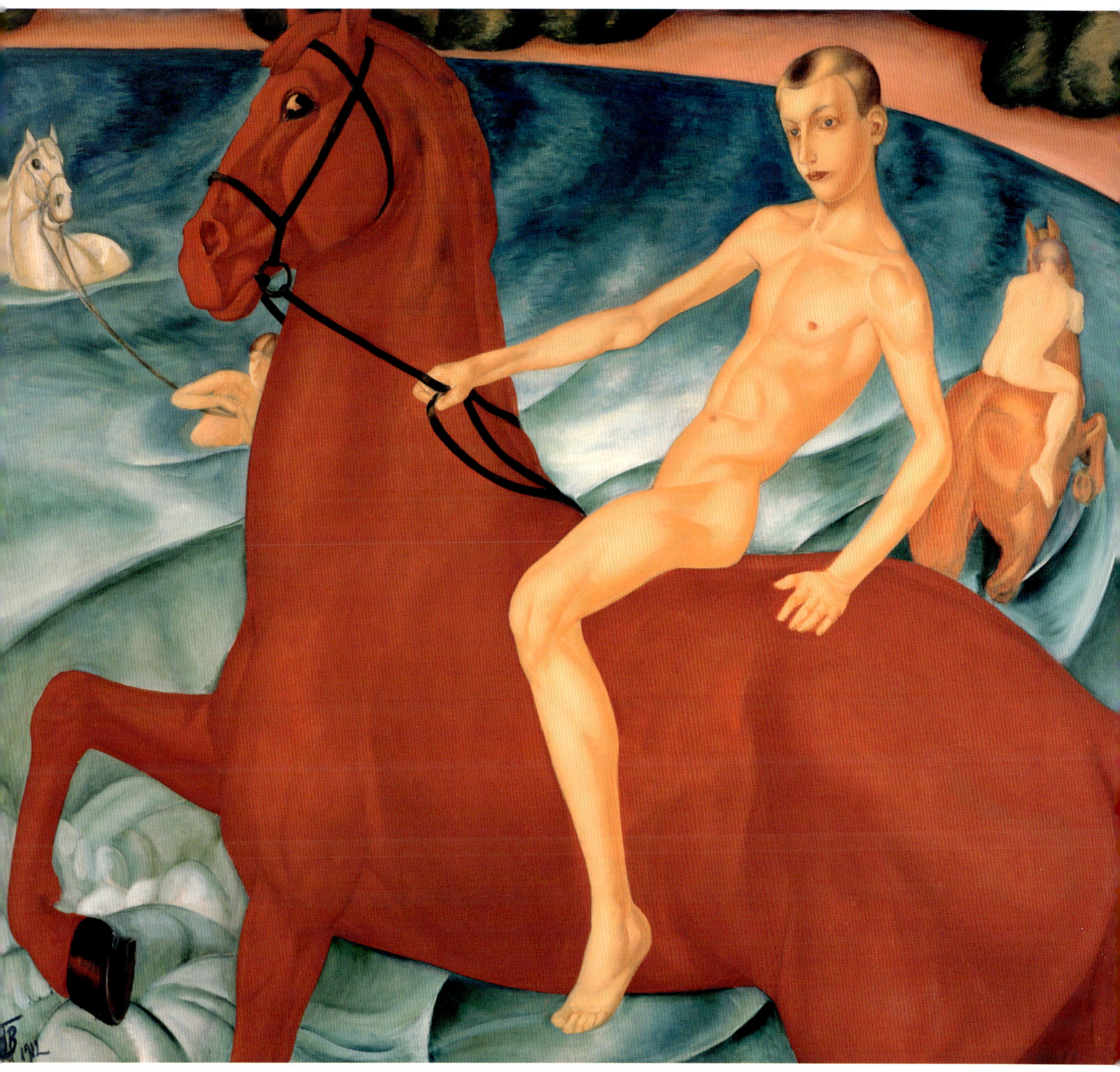
1912

Mikhail F. LARIONOV

1881 – 1964

Prostitute at the Hairdresser's. 1914
Oil on canvas. 59 x 58½ in.
(151,5 x 150 cm)
The State Tretyakov Gallery
Moscow, Russia

Mikhail Larionov was one of the leaders of the neo-primitive avant-garde movement in Russia at the beginning of the 20th century. In his folk art, reproduced and sold as inexpensive popular prints, Larionov did not distinguish between the high brow and the low brow or the beautiful and the ugly. The artist liked his characters and expressed an ironic attitude towards them. Prostitute at the Hairdresser's is one of the paintings belonging to what was called his "provincial" series. In that ironical and mocking canvas the artist addresses himself to the traditions of the lower culture of the town of Tiraspol where he was born.

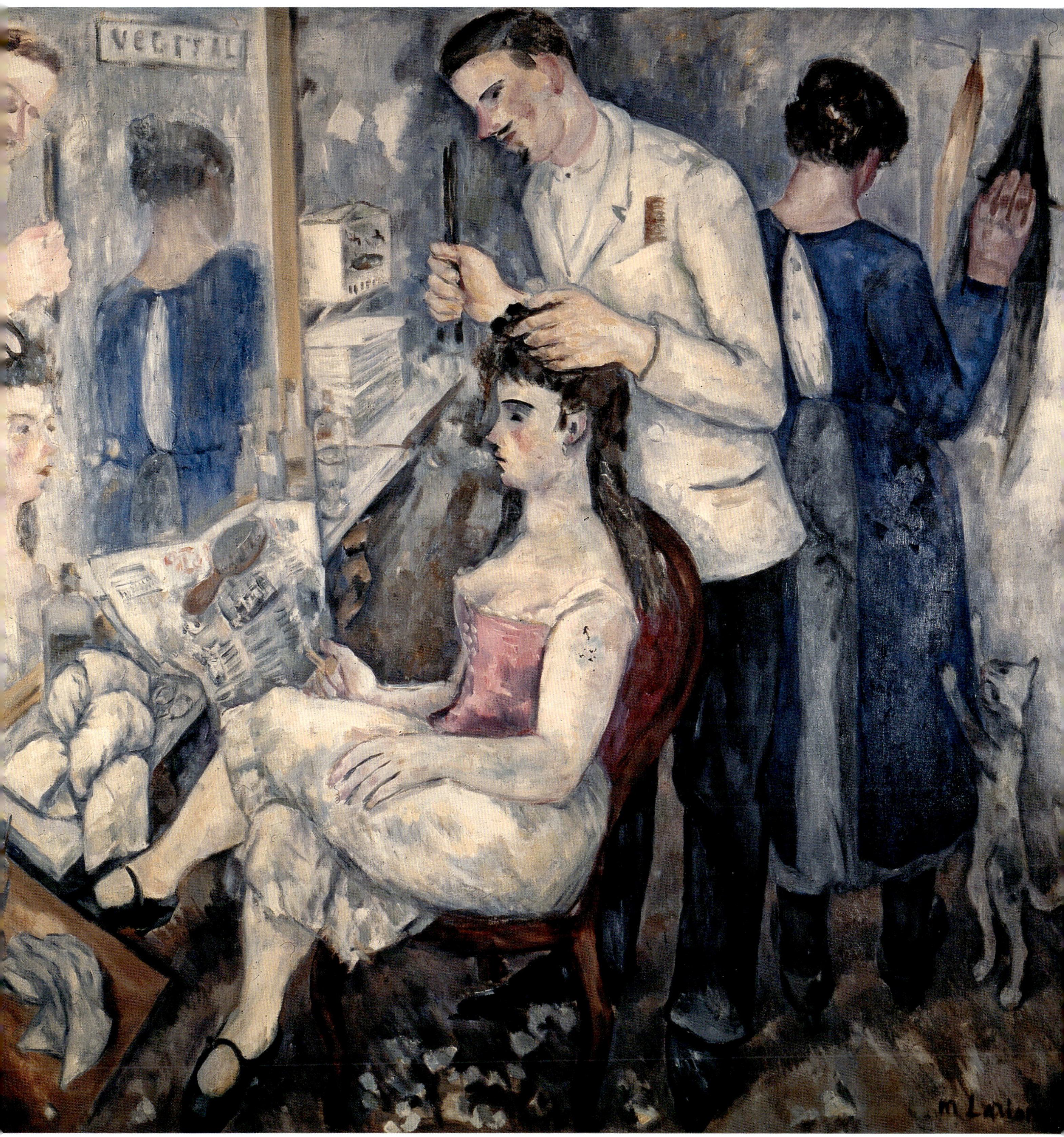

Aristarkh V. LENTULOV

1883 – 1943

Tower Gate. New Jerusalem. 1917
Oil on canvas. 39¾ x 38 in.
(101,9 x 97,3 cm.)
The State Tretyakov Gallery
Moscow, Russia

This painting is one in a series of Lentulov's most famous cubist-futuristic landscapes that depict Moscow's ancient Russian architecture, its historic towns and the monasteries surrounding it. The artist, fascinated by the theory of color and sound proximity, defines his artistic technique as "color dynamics."

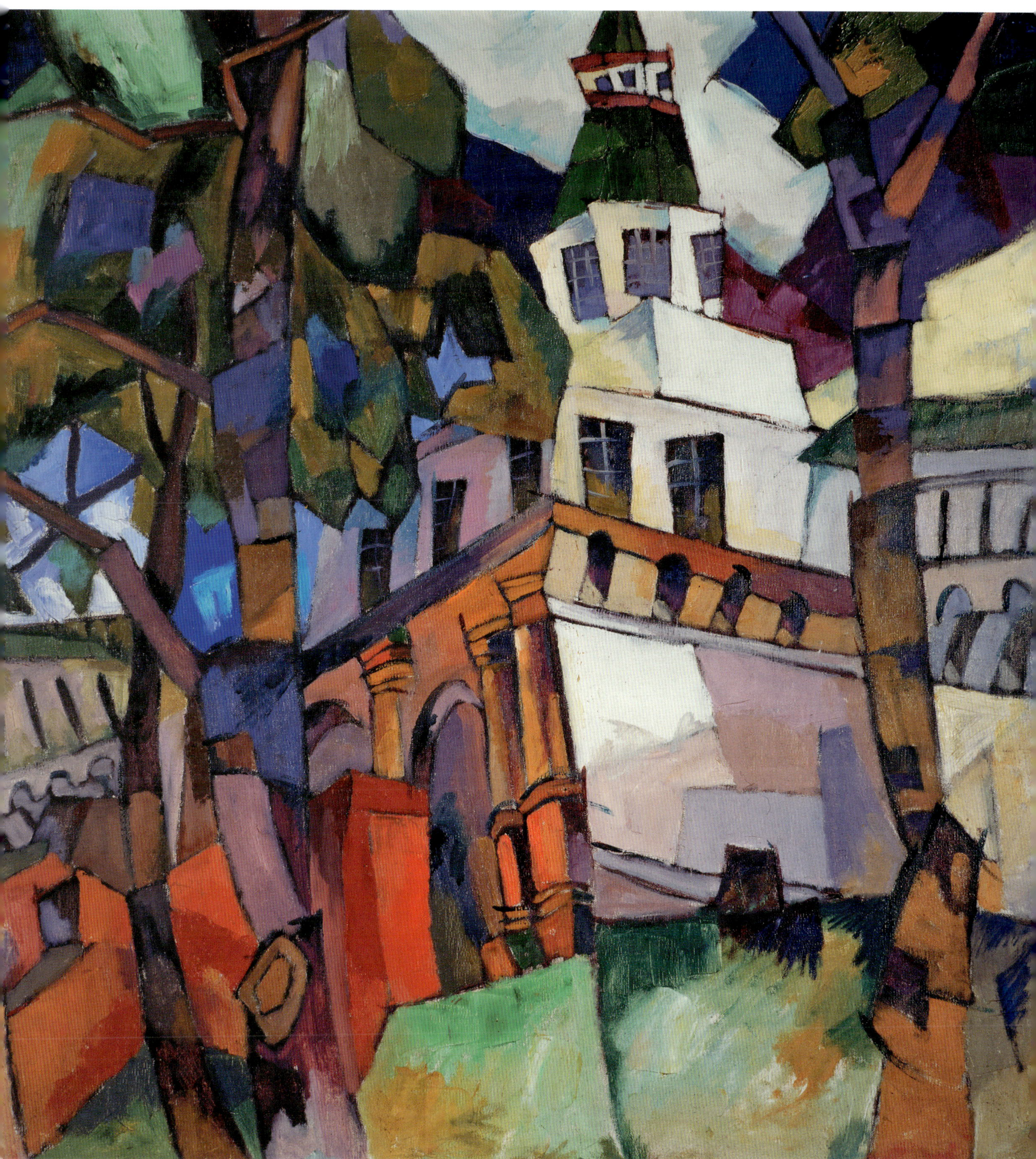

Vasili V. ROZHDESTVENSKI

1884 – 1963

Still Life With Green Bottle. 1921
Oil on canvas. 27¾ x 20¾ in.
(71 x 53 cm)
The State Tretyakov Gallery
Moscow, Russia

Rozhdestvenski was one of the founders, in the 1910s, of the Jack of Diamonds group of artists, which led the Russian avant-garde movement. Still Life With Green Bottle is an example of the blending of what became known as French Cezannism, Russian primitivism and cubism. In the 1920s and 1930s, Rozhdestvenski changed his focus, painting northern Russia and the Urals.

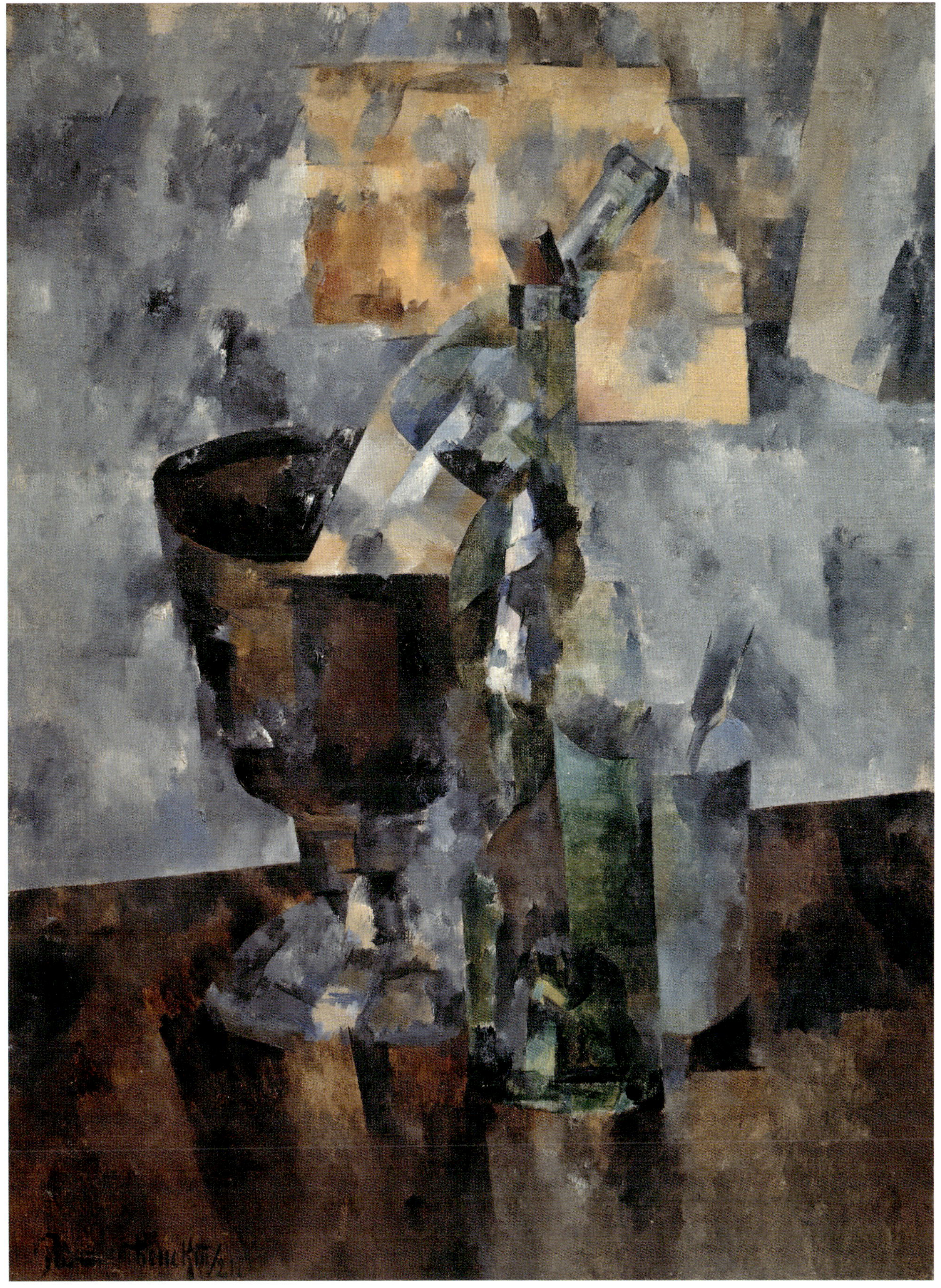

Konstantin F. YUON

1875 – 1958

Annunciation Day. 1922
Oil on canvas. 28½ x 39⅜ in.
(73 x 101 cm)
The State Tretyakov Gallery
Moscow, Russia

Yuon, a pupil of Valentin Serov, loved old Russian towns. In his Autobiography, he wrote: "The picturesque beauty of ancient Russian villages, with the activities of daily life lit by the sun's rays, allows me to escape from the monotonous colors of trivial...landscape art and gives me the full spectrum of lush, pure colors I love to use...."

This painting portrays the orthodox Annunciation holiday in the Troitse-Sergieva Lavra (Trinity-Sergiy Monastery) which is located on the outskirts of Moscow. Its shining golden cupolas and colorful, festive crowds instill in the spectator the joy of living.

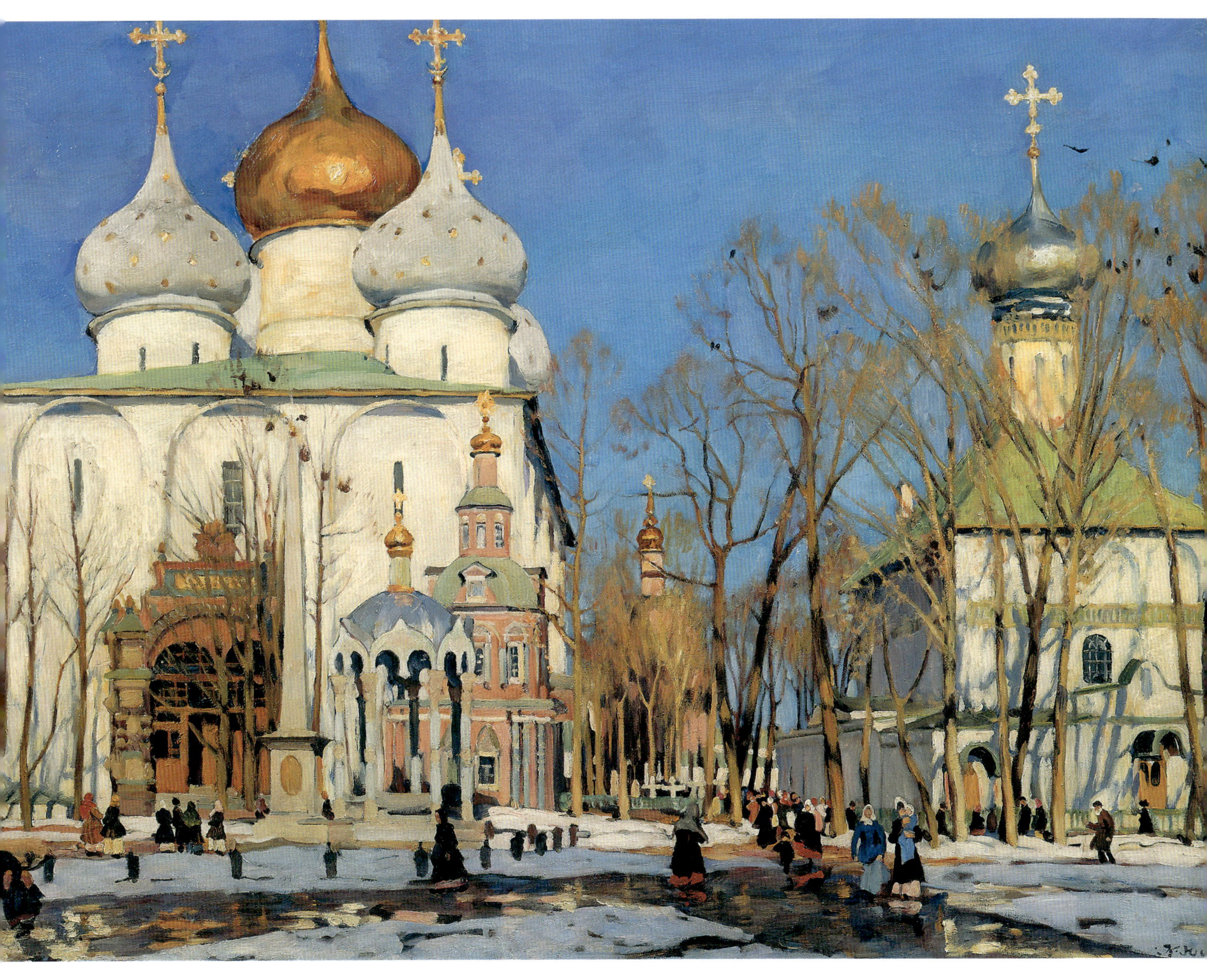

Robert R. FALK

1886 – 1958

Self Portrait. 1923
Oil on canvas. 32 x 26⅜ in.
(82 x 67,5 cm)
The State Tretyakov Gallery
Moscow, Russia

R. Falk came to Russian art with the famous Jack of Diamonds artists. Having paid his tribute to cubism, in the 1920s the artist addressed himself to his idea of looking at life. "Before starting work," he said, "I ponder many things; I think about the subject I am going to depict...the era, the landscape... I think about nursery rhymes and stories my grandmother told me as a child...And when I paint, I look at these things and see how much I have to be thankful for, what I once wished for and desired...."

In his Self Portrait, the artist is looking at himself and seeing the art he will paint in the future.

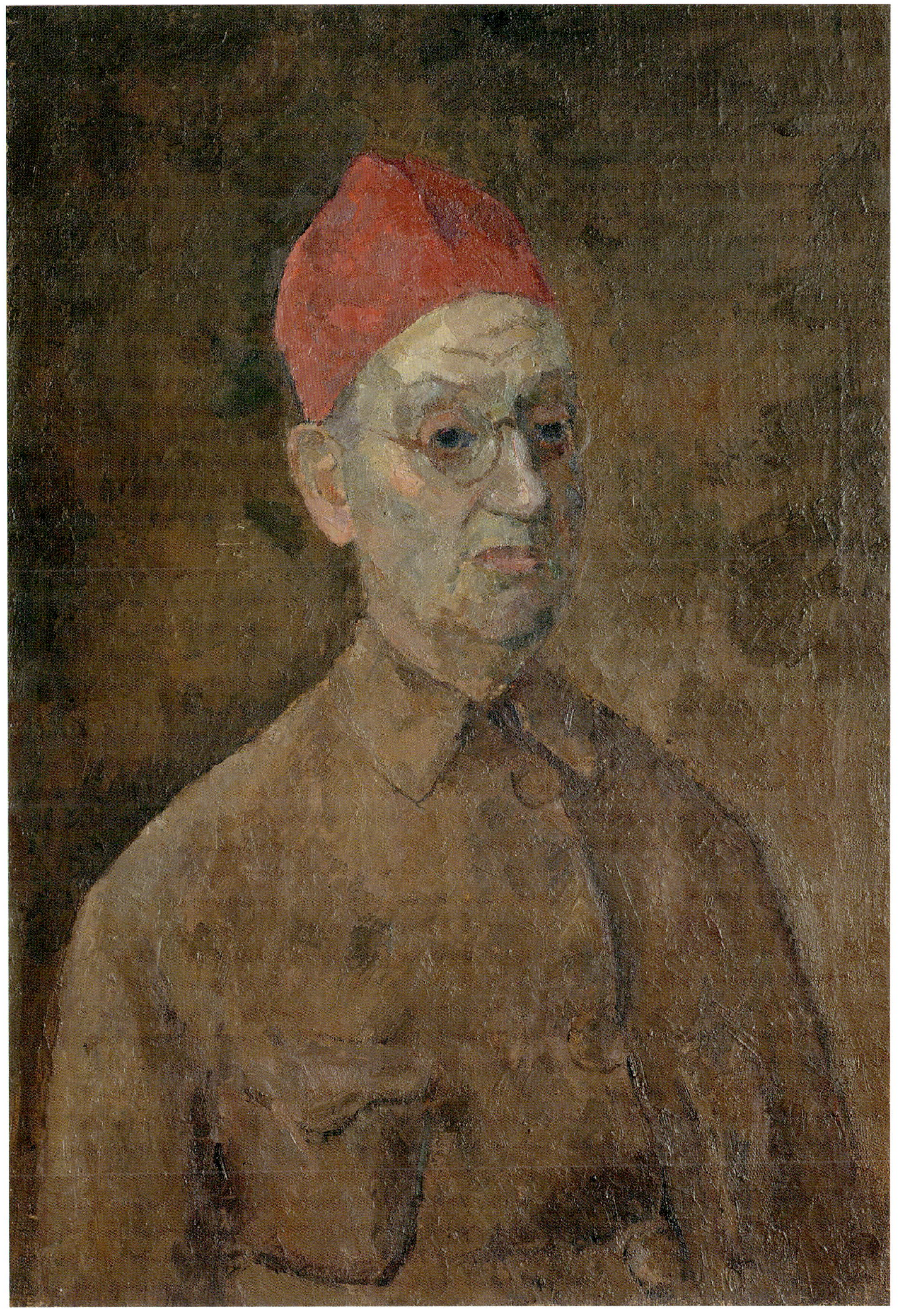

Aleksandr A. DEINEKA

1899 – 1969

Girl Sitting on a Chair. 1924
Oil on canvas. 46 x 28¼ in.
(118 x 72,5 cm)
The State Tretyakov Gallery
Moscow, Russia

Aleksandr Deineka is one of the outstanding figures in 20th century art. The artist introduced stylistic devices of posters, graphic art and monumental art into easel painting.

Girl Sitting on a Chair was painted as a spare image in what became his signature laconic graphic style. Deineka transforms a sharply defined character into a typical female image that is an image of the time.

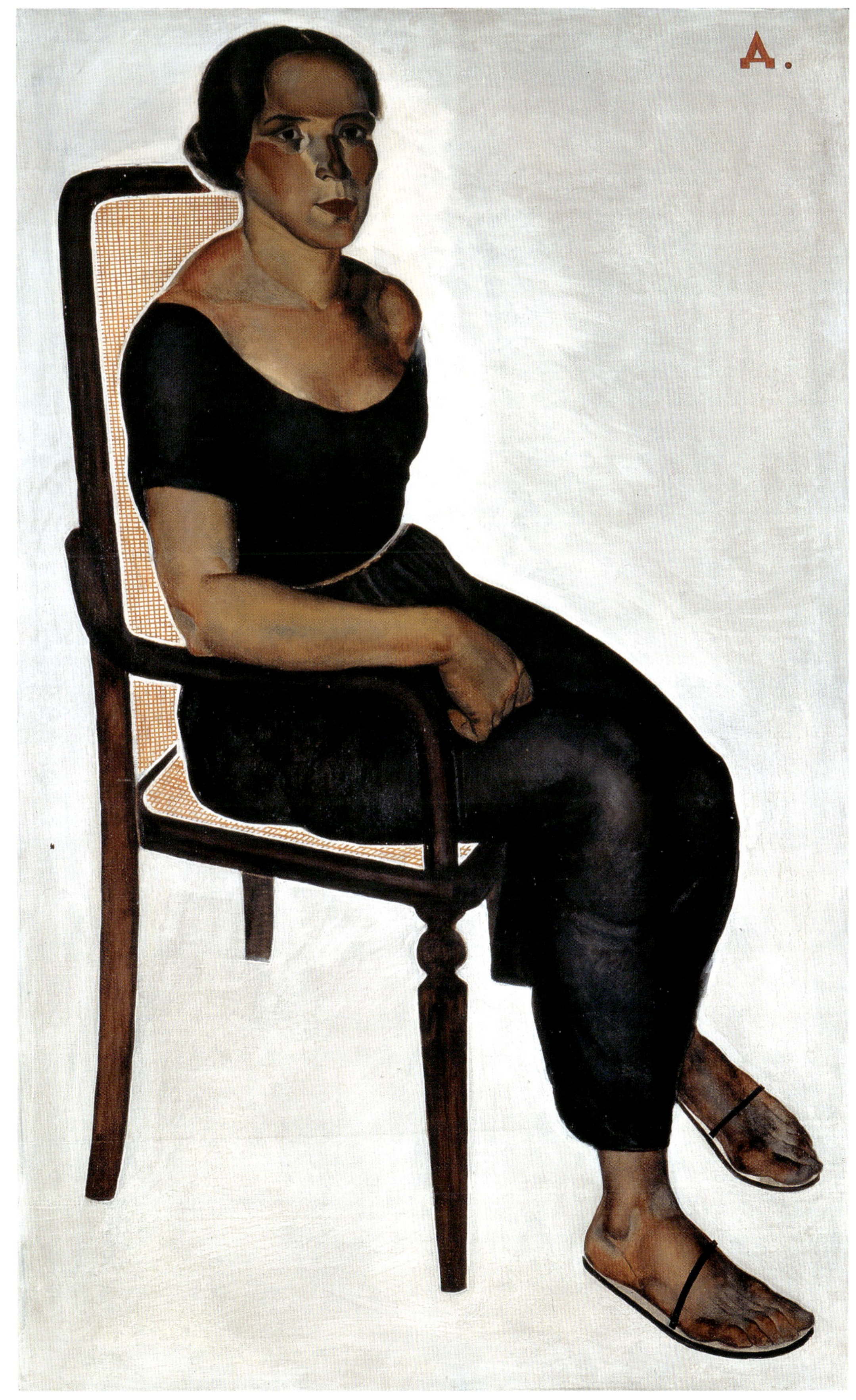
A.

Zinaida E. SERENBRYAKOVA

1884 – 1967

The Russian Bathhouse. 1926
Oil on canvas. 53½ x 31½ in.
(136 x 80 cm)
From a Private American Collection
Loan arranged by
The Museum of Russian Art
Minneapolis, Minnesota USA

Zinaida Serebryakova belonged to the famous Benois–Lansere art dynasty. Her art is an example of Russian neoclassicism of the first half of the 20th century. The Russian Bathhouse, with its fluid forms, impressive silhouettes and restrained colors, is a vivid example of Serebryakova's classical art.

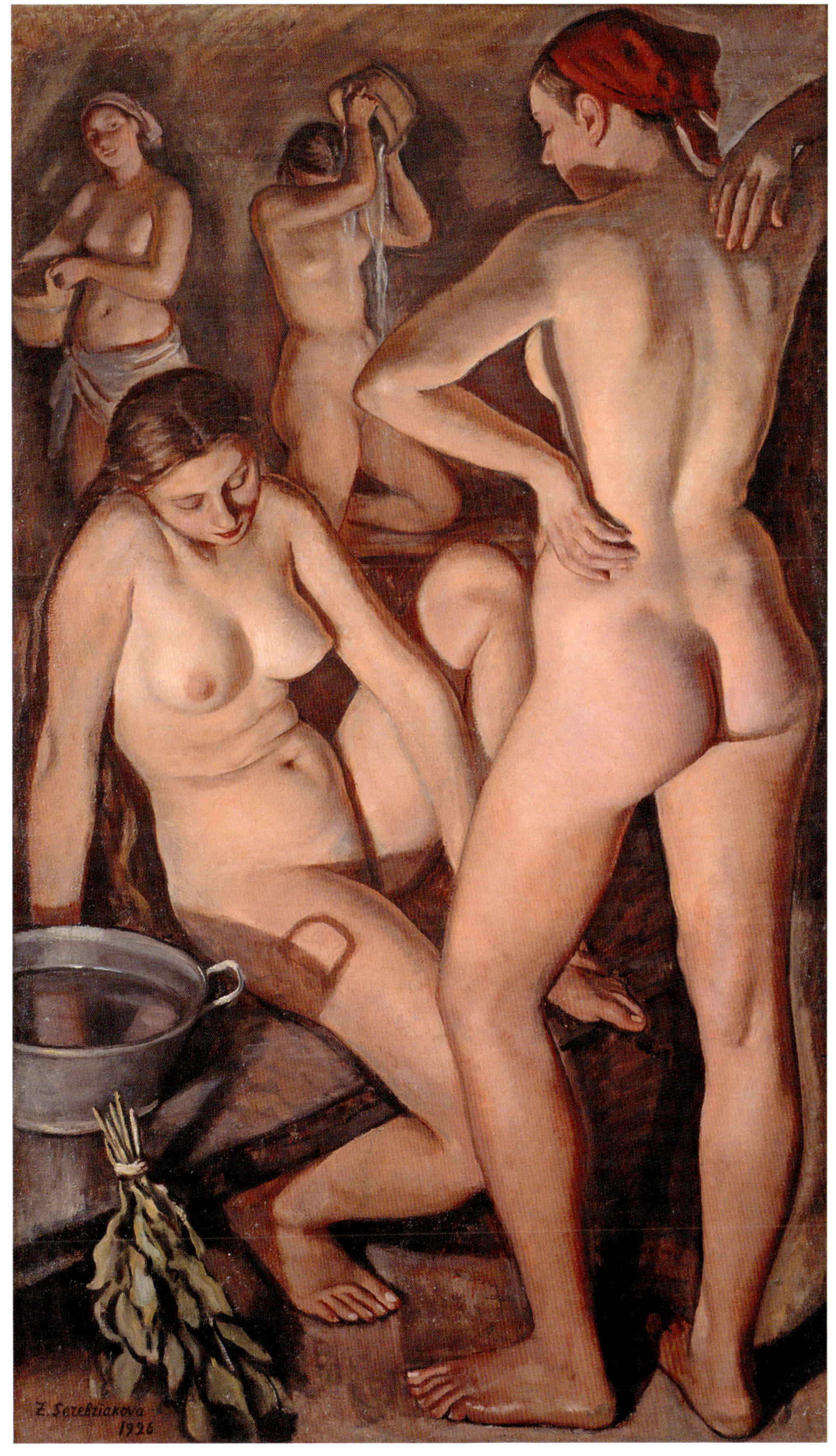
Z. Serebriakova
1926

Yuri I. PIMENOV

1903 – 1977

Chinese Theatre. 1928
Oil on canvas. 46 x 70½ in.
(116,8 x 179 cm)
From a Private American Collection
Loan arranged by
The Museum of Russian Art
Minneapolis, Minnesota USA

Chinese Theatre belongs to the artist's early period when he was strongly influenced by German expressionism. His incongruous artistic language and desire to shock the viewer are seen in the costumes, poses and movements of the actors depicted in the painting.

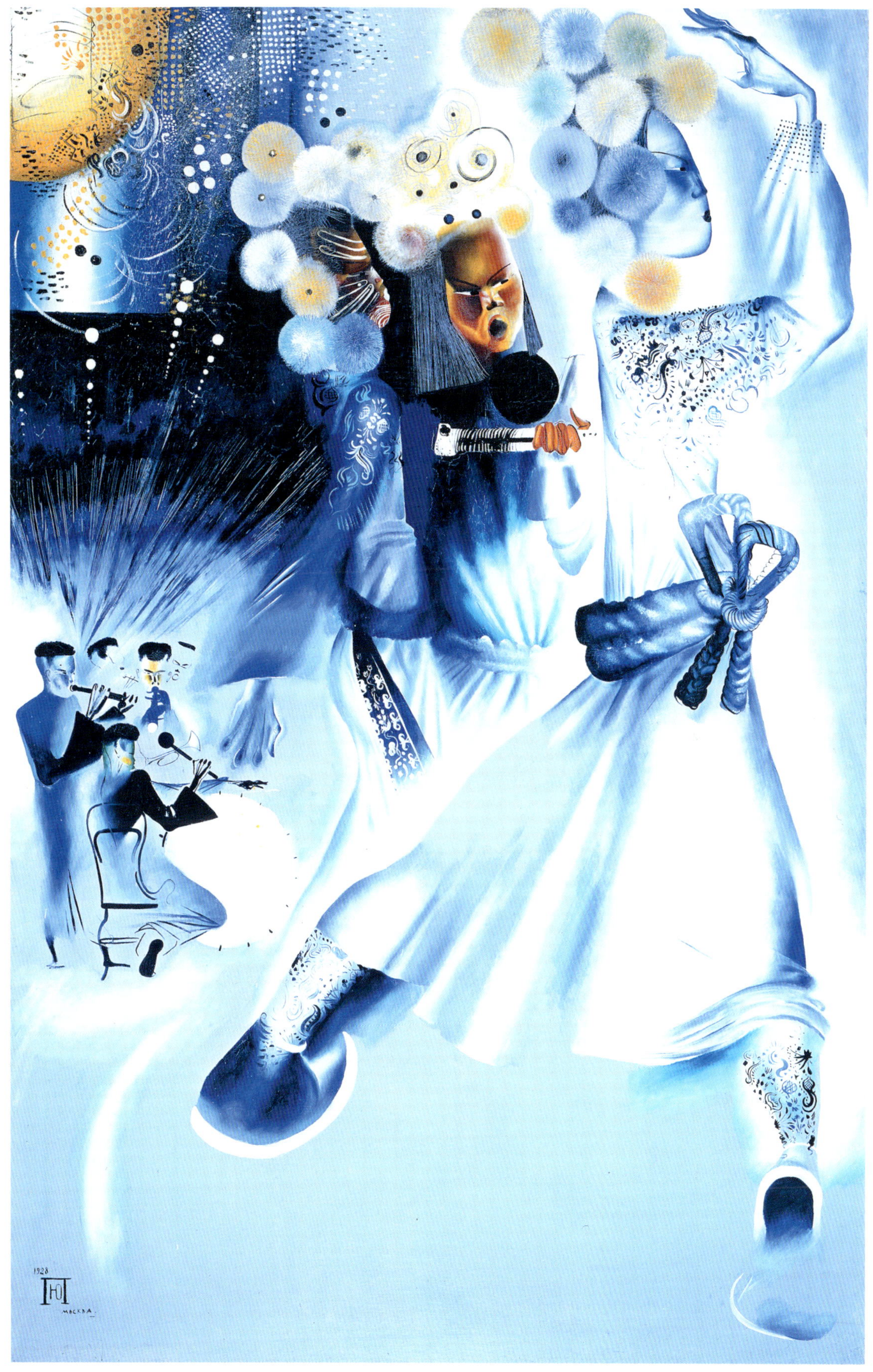
1928
МОСКВА

Aleksandr M. GERASIMOV

1881 – 1963

Trees In Bloom. 1930s
Oil on canvas. 49 x 52½ in.
(124 x 133 cm)
From a Private American Collection
Loan arranged by
The Museum of Russian Art
Minneapolis, Minnesota USA

In his works painted during the 1930s and 1940s, the artist demonstrates the art traditions he inherited from Ilya Repin and his teacher, Valentin Serov. The motif of apple trees in blossom is quite characteristic of Gerasimov's works from 1910 to the 1950s. Many times the artist returned to his earlier works, changing them and painting them again and again.

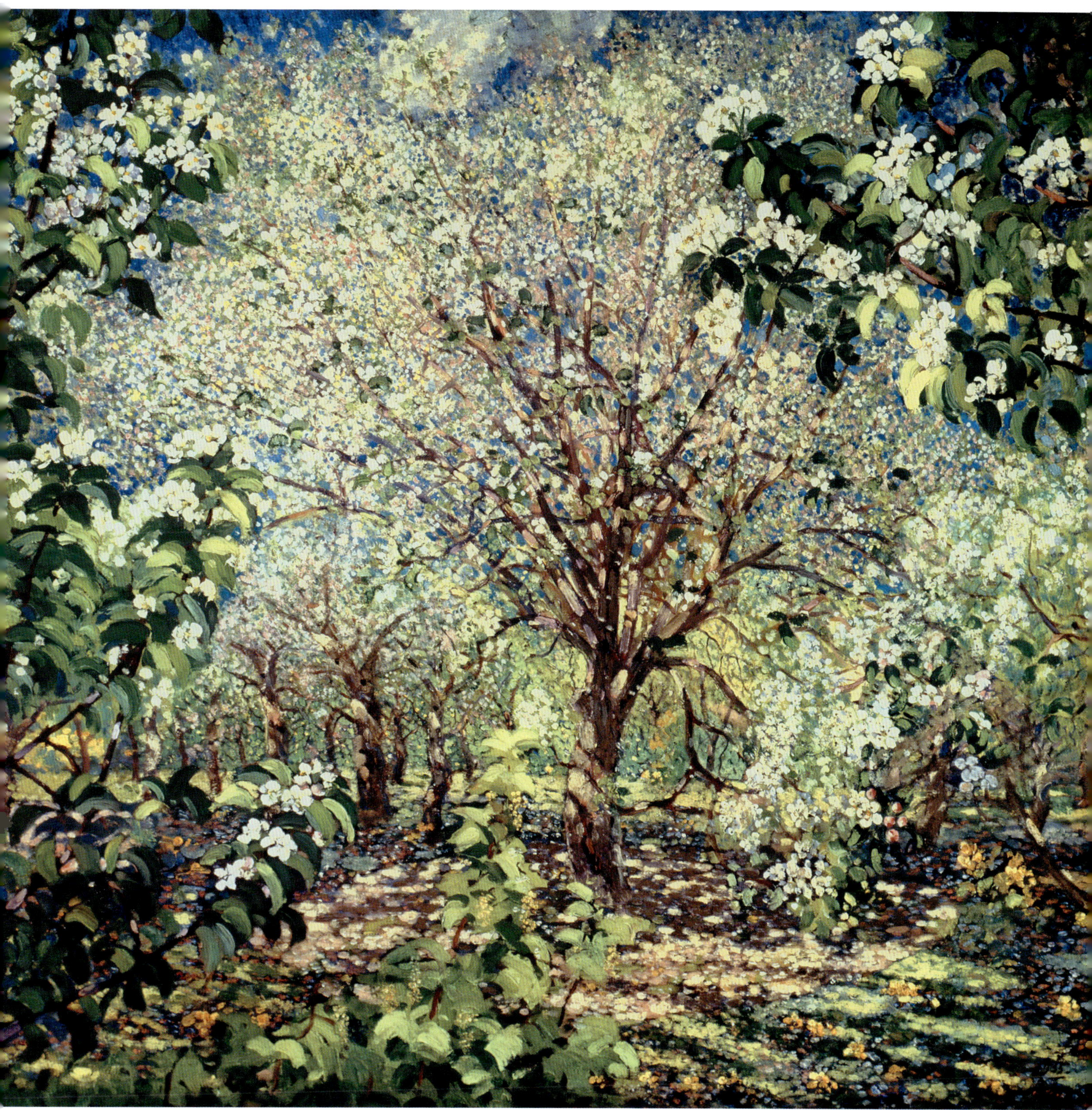

Petr V. WILLIAMS

1902 – 1947

Nana (Woman at the Table). 1934
Oil on canvas. 31½ x 40½ in.
(81 x 104 cm)
The State Tretyakov Gallery
Moscow, Russia

An artist who was fascinated by people, Williams was connected with the theater throughout his life. His theatrical portraits were created on the attractiveness, originality and artistry of his models. This portrait combines the characteristics of one of Zola's literary characters with the essence of the life model. Together they become a single entity, inviting the viewer into their light, carnival atmosphere.

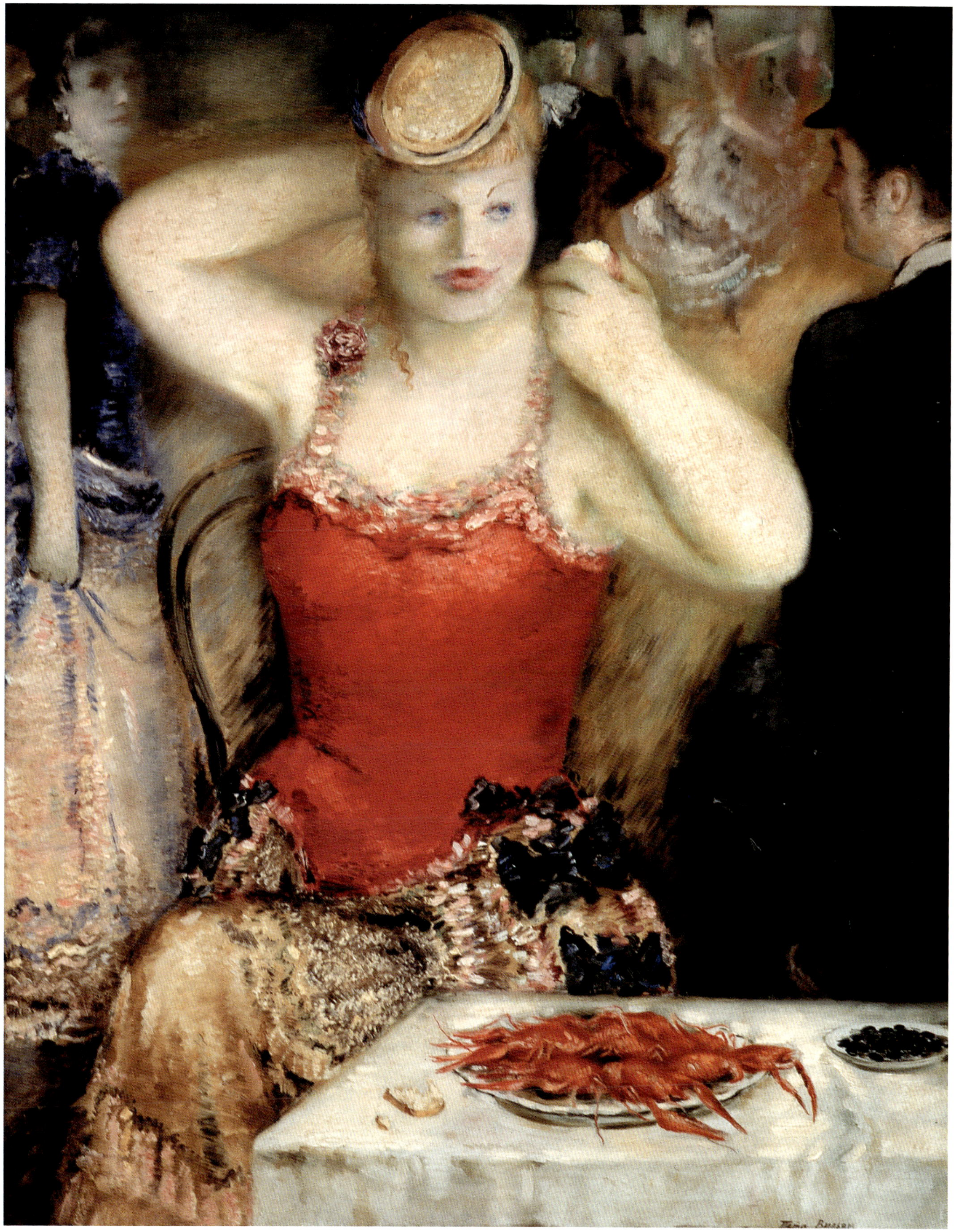

Boris N. YAKOVLEV

1890–1972

Soviet Canned Food. 1939
Oil on canvas. 53⅞ x 63⅛ in.
(138 x 162 cm)
The State Tretyakov Gallery
Moscow, Russia

Boris Yakovlev's works were included in the last exhibitions of the Union of Russian Artists in the 1920s. He was one of the creators of the Soviet industrial landscape. In his still life Soviet Canned Food the artist created an homage to Soviet industry.

Admiration for the still life – a receptacle of life – is quite specific to the Russian painting tradition of the 20th century.

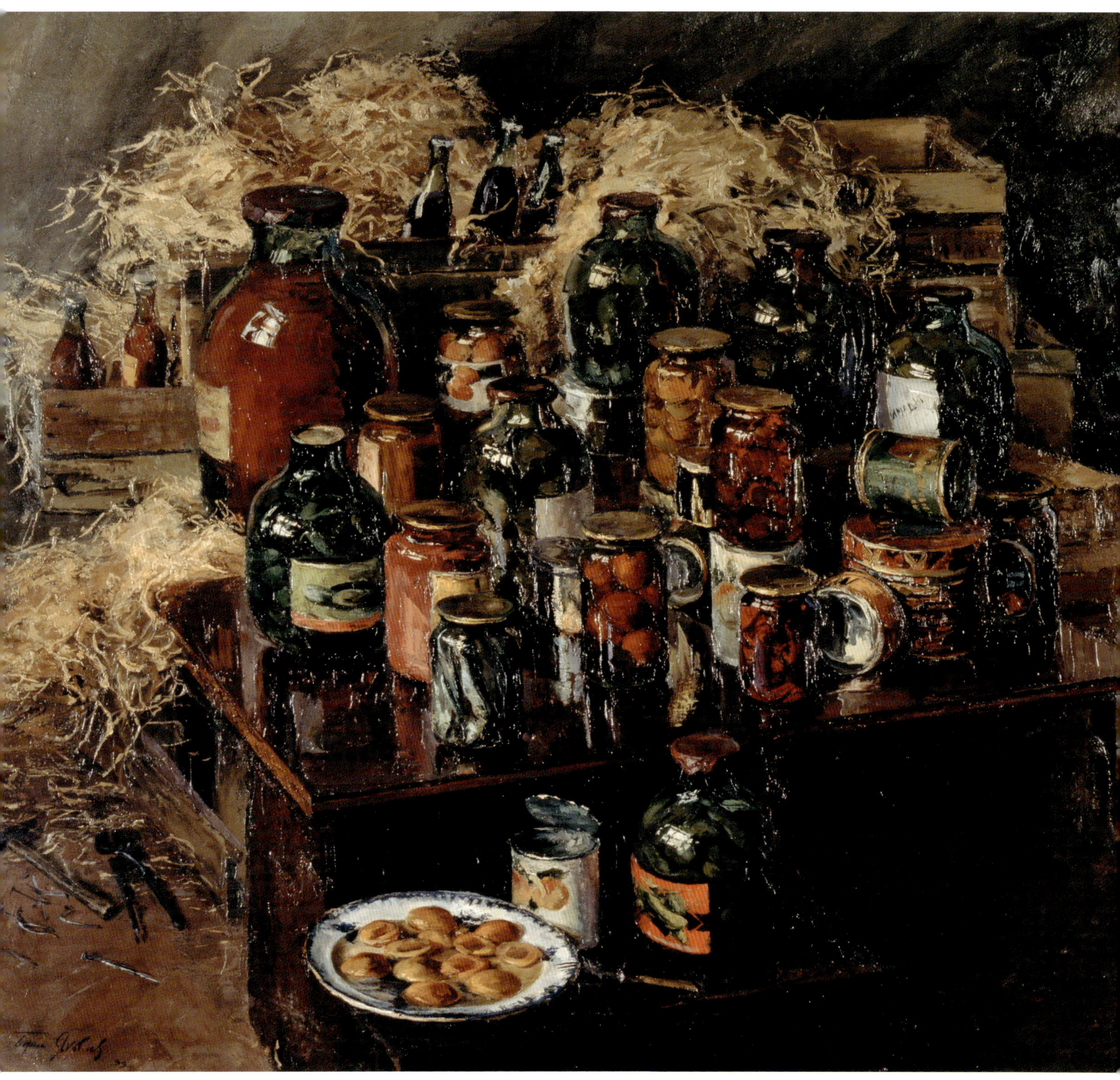

Petr P. KONCHALOVSKI

1876 – 1956

Floor-Polisher. 1946
Oil on canvas. 66⅝ x 55¾ in.
(171 x 143 cm)
The State Tretyakov Gallery
Moscow, Russia

Vladimir Pereyaslavets (born in 1918), who is now a well-known Moscow artist, sat for Floor-Polisher.

A bright founding member of the famous Jack of Diamonds group, Petr Konchalovski was devoted to an open, colorful manner of execution that he learned in his youth. In one of his later works, Floor-Polisher, the artist revels in producing combinations of bright red, dark green and golden colors as if remembering the French post-impressionistic experience that so influenced his youth.

Konchalovski strove to create vivid impressions in his art. The artist wrote: "Life itself gives me subjects for my paintings, just as the visible world does: that's why I dislike invented compositions. A contrived plot is not welcome in my art.... What is important to me is to see beauty in daily phenomena and to find a great style in order to express that beauty..."

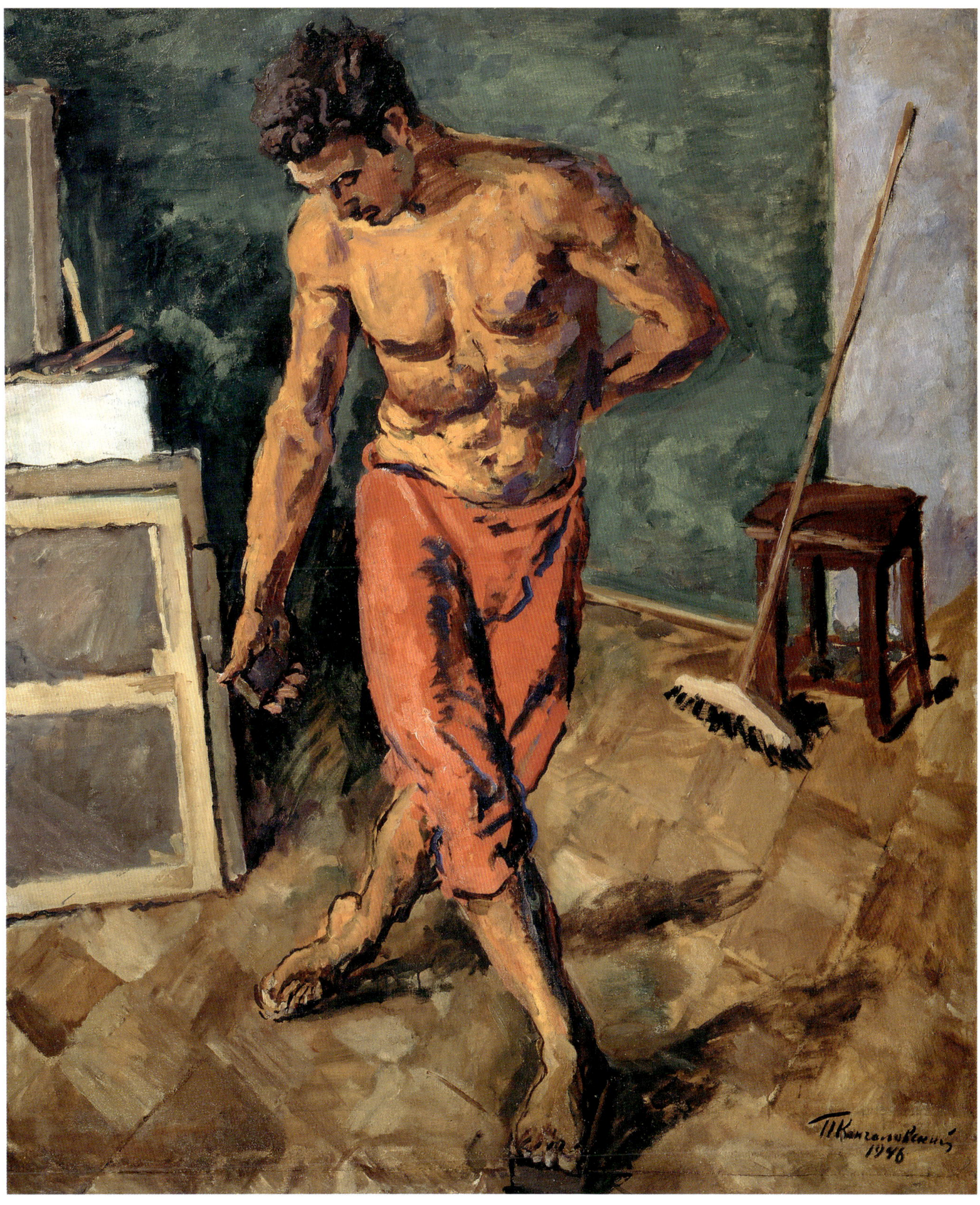
ПКончаловский
1946

Nikolai M. ROMADIN

1903 – 1987

Black Lake. 1946
Oil on Whatman paper.
22⅝ x 32⅜ in.
(58 x 83 cm)
The State Tretyakov Gallery
Moscow, Russia

Romadin's art continues the traditions of Russian lyrical landscape painting in the second half of the 20th century. According to Konstantin Paustovski, the artist's contemporary: "Just by looking at the painting one can become chilled; feel the wind, the river's icy breath, soaked through by the rain; and smell the needles of pungent fir trees."

This landscape was painted in the dense woods of Kerzhenets, a village on the bank of the lower Volga River, which often overflows in the spring. The theme of the flooded forest, with a blazing sunset bathing the tree trunks in brilliant scarlet, attracted the artist. Nearly all the men of Kerzhenets perished there during World War II. With that in mind, Romadin painted a natural disaster, employing the starkness of black and white.

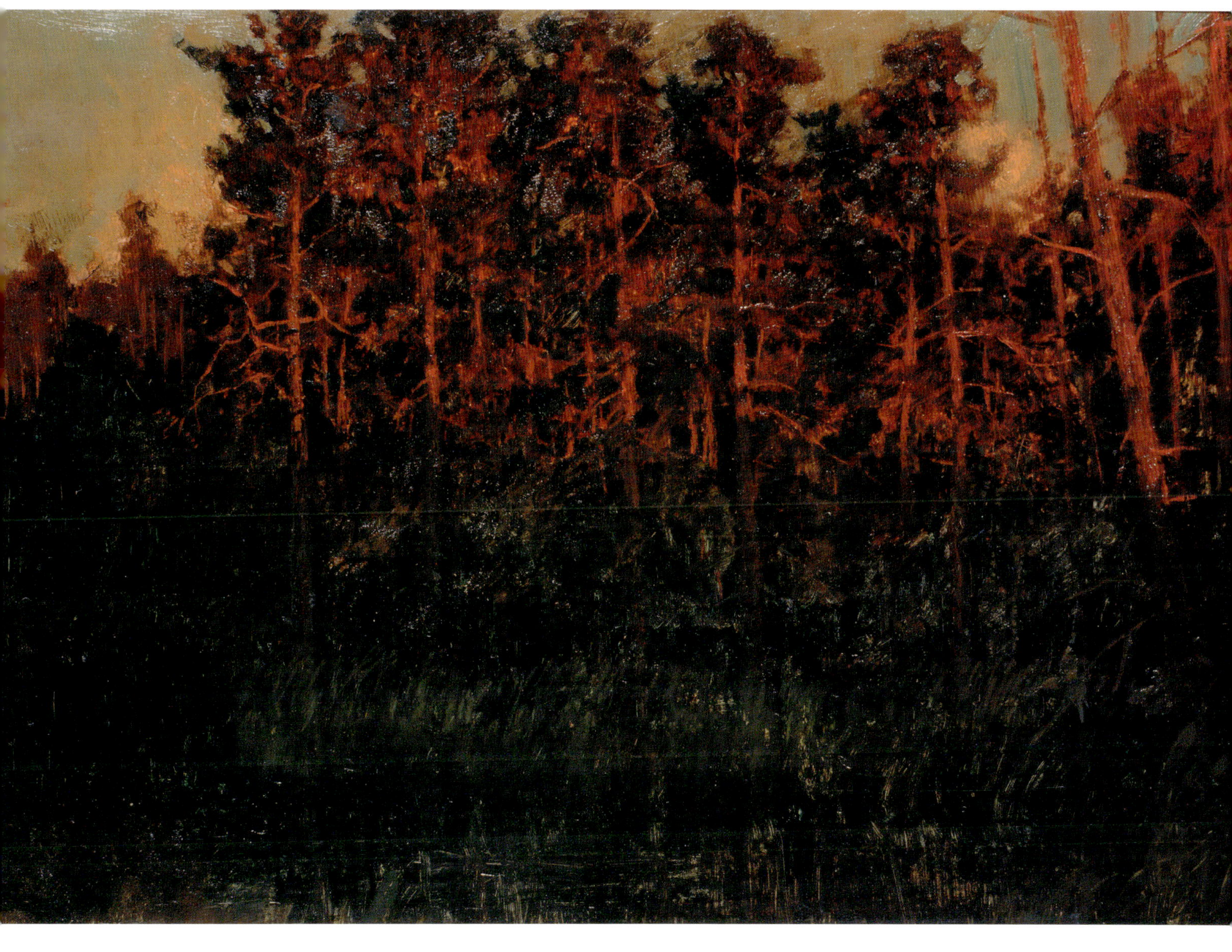

Gavril N. GORELOV

1880 – 1966

Portrait of a Boy. 1947
Oil on canvas. 39¼ x 22⅛ in.
(99,7 x 56,2 cm)
From a Private American Collection
Loan arranged by
The Museum of Russian Art
Minneapolis, Minnesota USA

Gorelov was a unique custodian of the Repin portrait tradition in mid-20th century art. Repin's influence on the young painter was pronounced. "I admired him immensely. Even brief comments and ideas from Ilya Efimovich gave me clear direction," Gorelov once recounted. In this painting there is truthfulness and a certain freedom in Gorelov's style–almost an incompleteness in the image–that makes Portrait of a Boy a masterpiece of our time.

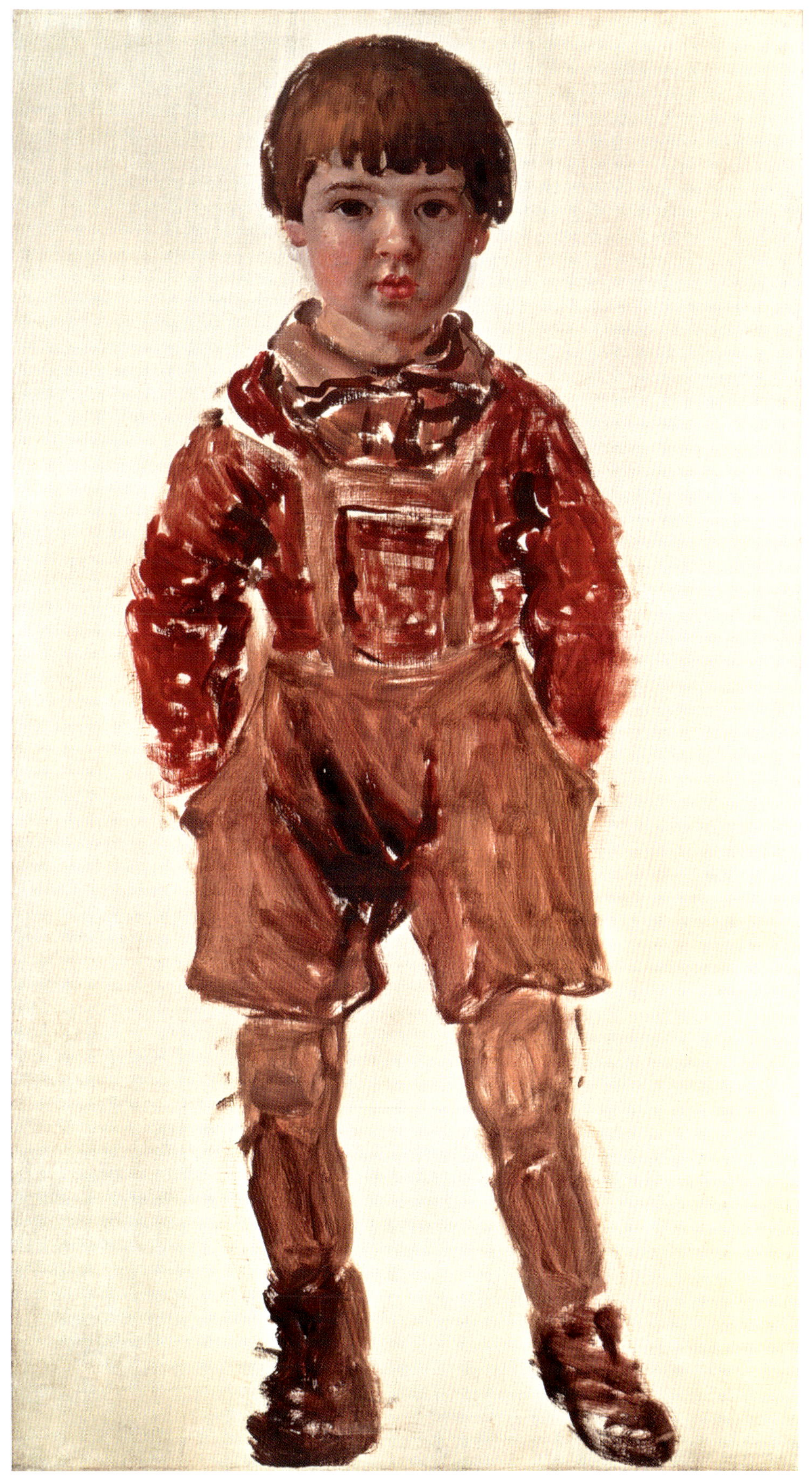

Zinaida M. KOVALEVSKAYA

1902 – 1979

Tomato Picking. 1949
Oil on canvas. 67 x 79 in.
(150 x 180 cm)
From a Private American Collection
Loan arranged by
The Museum of Russian Art
Minneapolis, Minnesota USA

Zinaida Kovalevskaya, a pupil of Nikolai Fechin, lived all her life in the Soviet Republic of Uzbekistan. A master of genre topics and a remarkable artist, in Tomato Picking she addressed the theme of abundance and happiness in post-war life. With an associate, Pavel Benkov, she established the first art school in Samarkand.

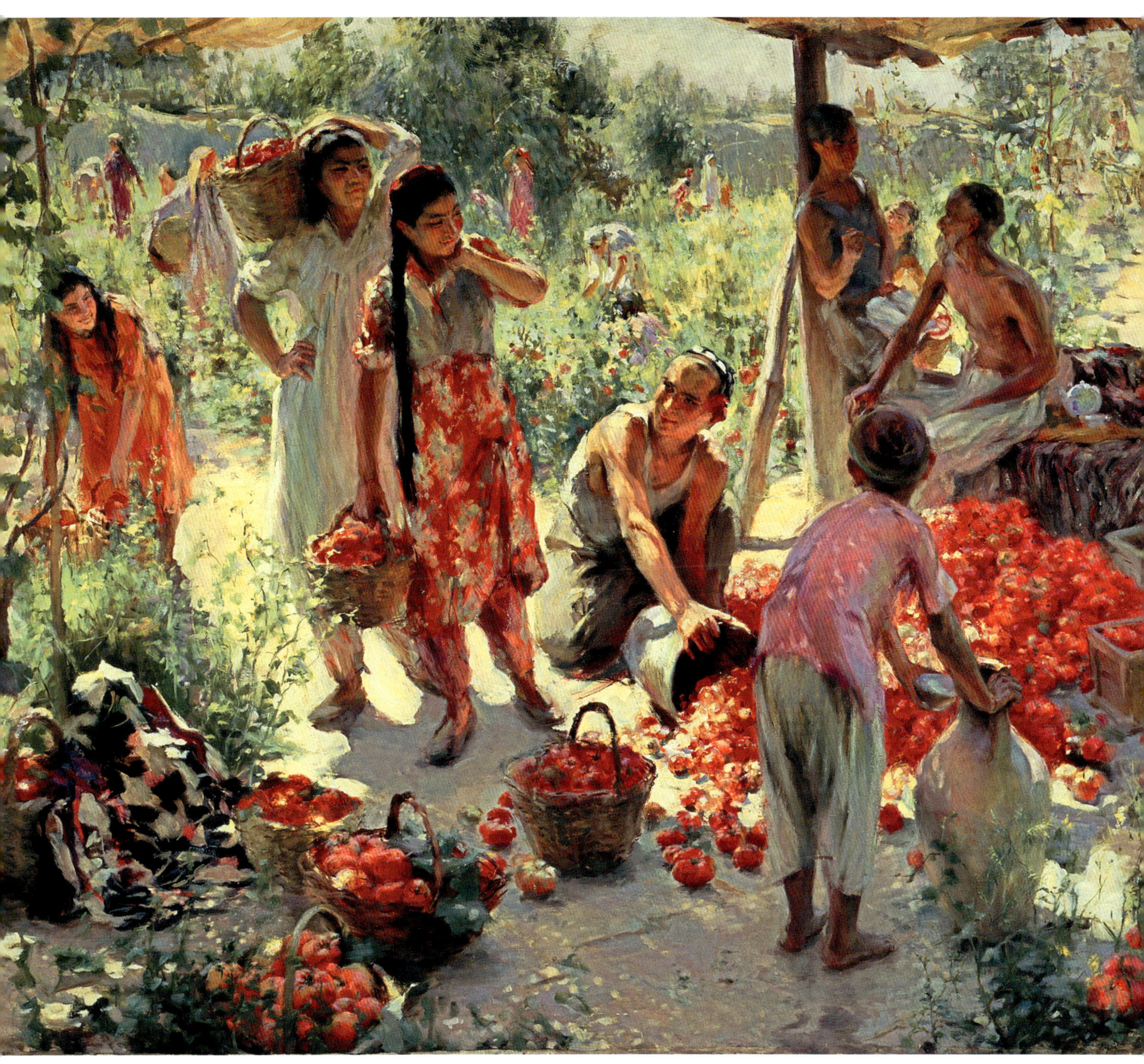

Sergei V. GERASIMOV

1885 – 1964

Evening. 1950
Oil on canvas. 31 x 39 in.
(79 x 99 cm)
From a Private American Collection
Loan arranged by
The Museum of Russian Art
Minneapolis, Minnesota USA

Sergei Gerasimov, an outstanding Russian painter with a passion for landscapes and a student of Konstantin Korovin, was reminiscing at the end of his life. "I remember my first lesson in Korovin's studio," he said. "My first etude (study) was a failure.... And, I do remember my last lesson. I had passed the course at the Moscow School of Painting, Sculpture and Architecture and had graduated from Korovin's studio. Konstantin Alexeyevich said impatiently: 'Enough, enough, go into the street, paint people, animals, the sun... everything, yes everything that impresses you in life.'

"The major themes of my work are the life of my people and my motherland...."

(S.V. Gerasimov. About Art. Moscow, 1973, page 100)

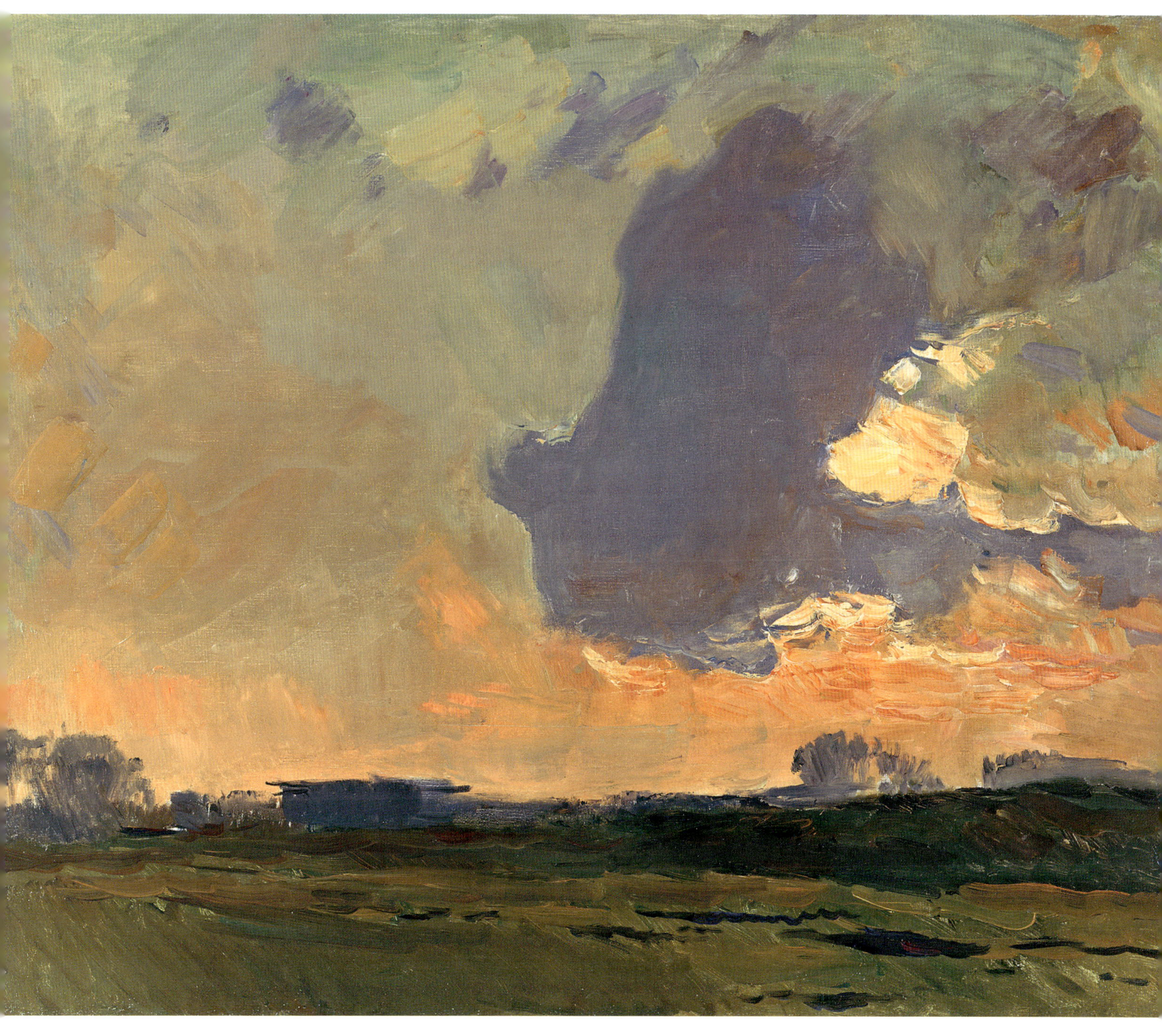

Yuri L. KATTS

1915 – 1988

Still Life. 1950s.
Oil on canvas. 31¼ x 45½ in.
(79,4 x 115,6 cm)
From a Private American Collection
Loan arranged by
The Museum of Russian Art
Minneapolis, Minnesota USA

Katts is a rare Soviet art master of traditional still life painting. The artist enjoyed depicting each object in exquisite detail–colorful patterns on a snowy white tablecloth, the lushness of fresh fruits–working with painstaking care with each brushstroke. Katts wrote: "I strive to paint as close to life as possible, and I am always sorry if I miss anything at all that is in the image, from its essence to its most subtle nuance...."

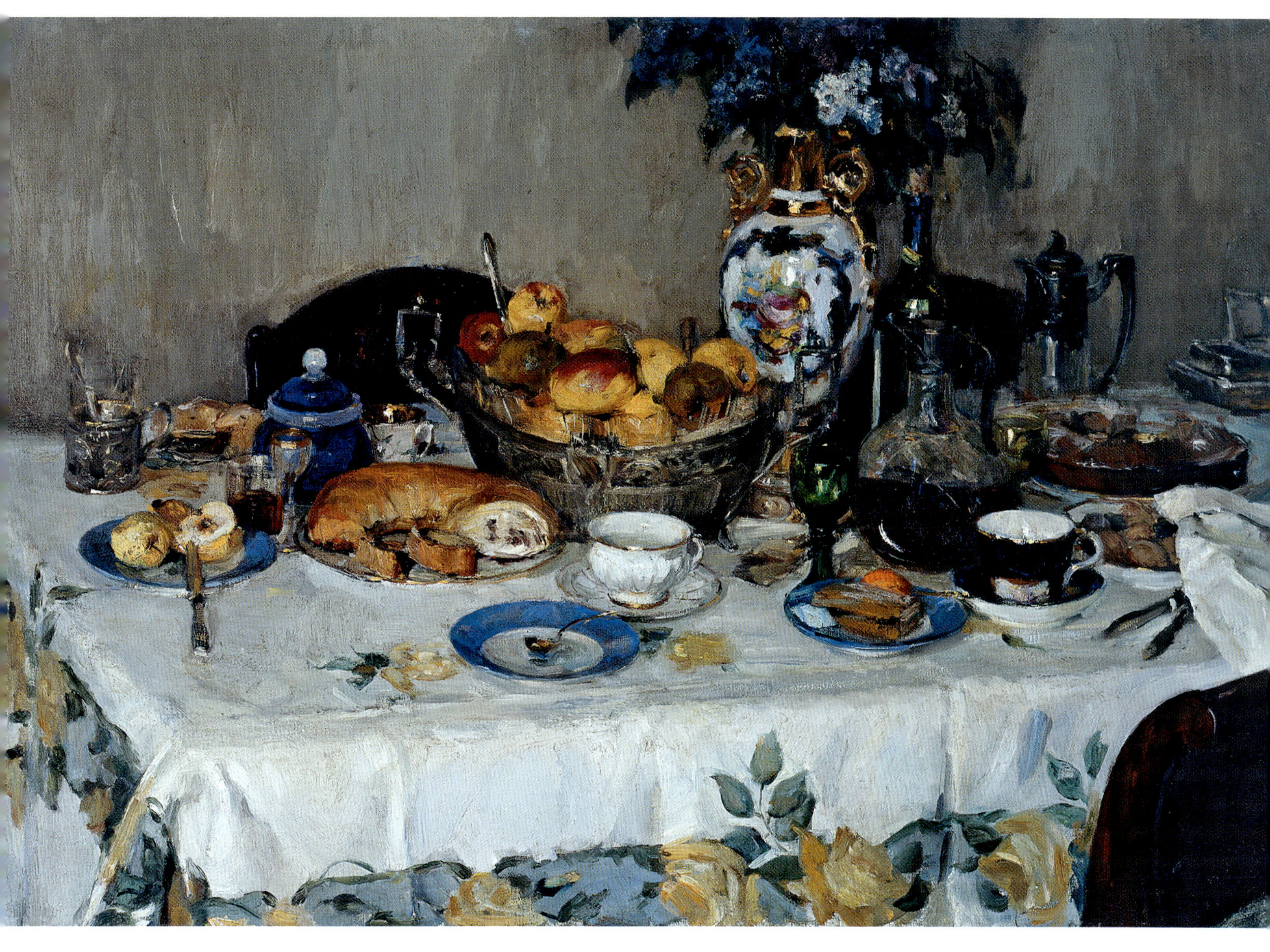

Aleksei P. TKACHEV

Born in 1925

Sergei P. TKACHEV

Born in 1922

The Post Girl in Winter. 1951
Oil on canvas. 50 x 38 in.
(127 x 96,5 cm)
From a Private American Collection
Loan arranged by
The Museum of Russian Art
Minneapolis, Minnesota USA

Tamara Kodykova, the artists' niece, is depicted in this painting.

In an interview, the Tkachev brothers, who are noted for often painting on the same canvas, credited their teachers with inspiring their work. "Such teachers as Sergei Gerasimov cultivated in us an impressionistic vision of the world as well as our love of color, which always lives in our works.... Our paintings tell our life stories. The subjects are not fantasies, they all spring from real people, real events and from stories told to us by our elders. Part of our souls are in each one."

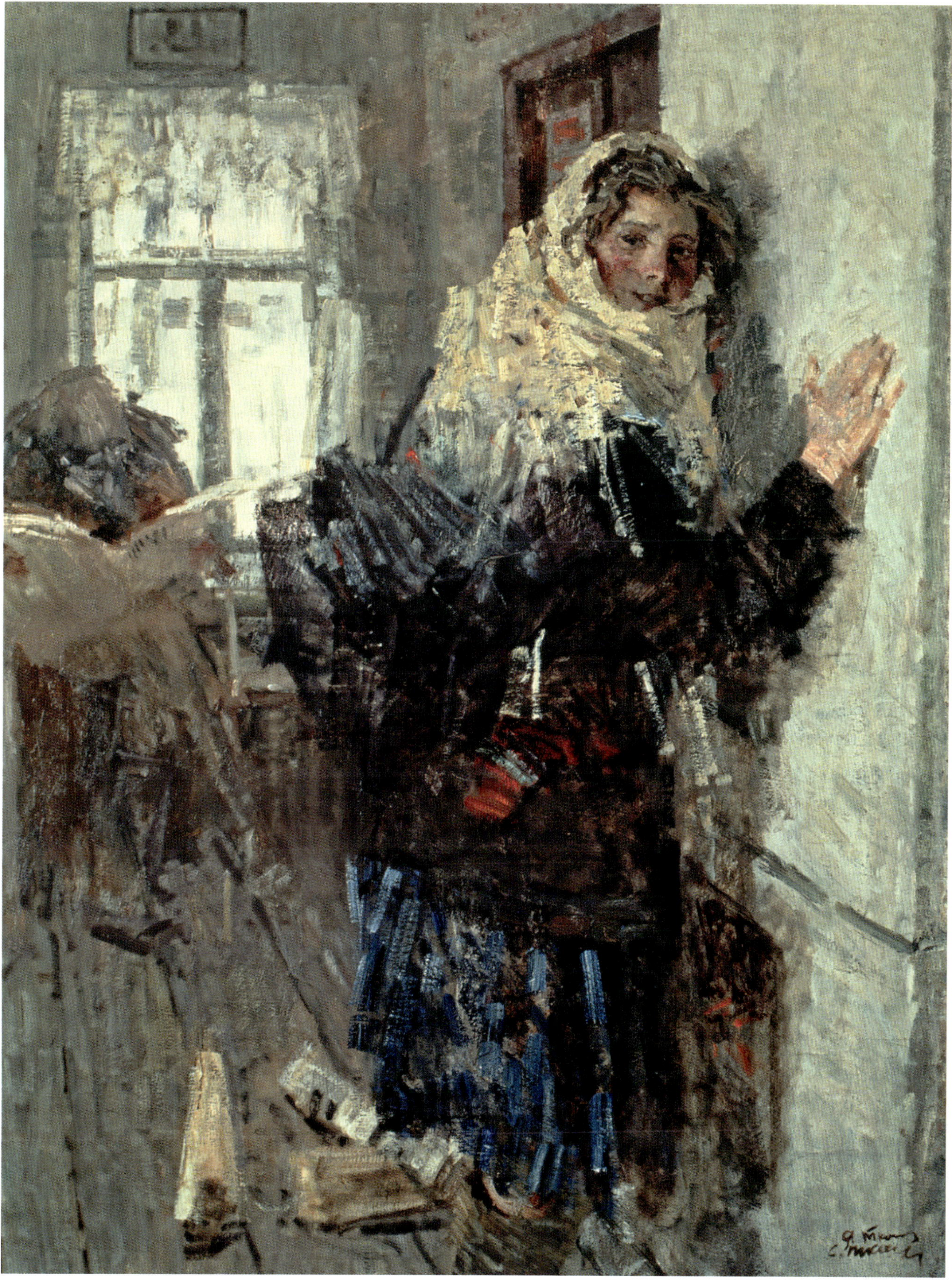

Oleg L. LOMAKIN

Born in 1924

Road Worker. Nina. 1954
Oil on canvas. 57 x 36 in.
(145 x 91cm)
From a Private American Collection
Loan arranged by
The Museum of Russian Art
Minneapolis, Minneapolis USA

The artist met this young woman, working with a road crew, in the street and asked her to model for this genre portrait. Wearing a quilted jacket and mittens, she symbolizes the beauty of youth. In his biography he noted, "I love to paint interesting people...I have painted many subjects, but portraits are my favorite form of expression. The sense of life...is indispensable in painting...."

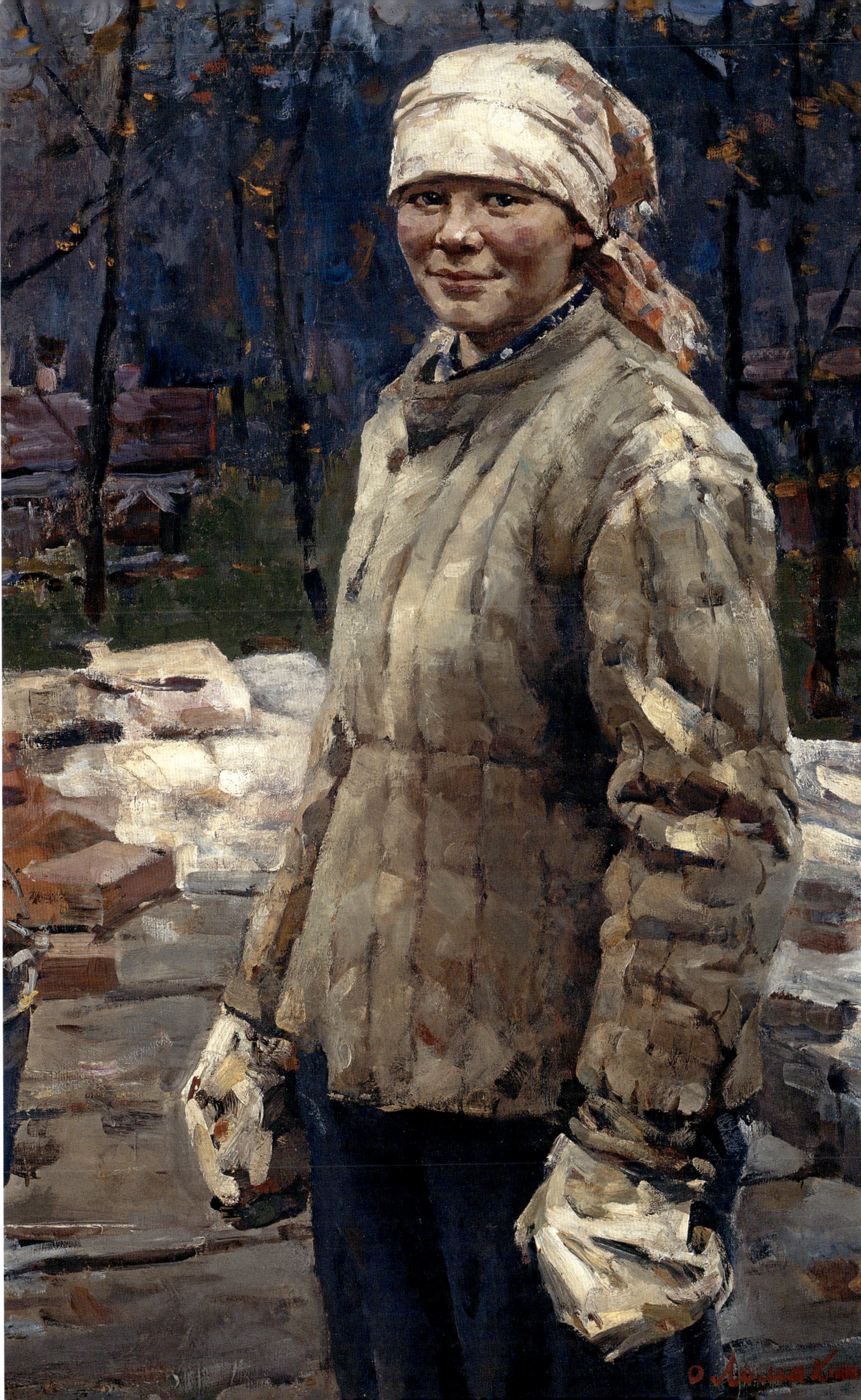

Boris S. UGAROV

1922 – 1991

Ginger Horse. 1954
Oil on board. 21 x 30½ in.
(54 x 78 cm)
The State Tretyakov Gallery
Moscow, Russia

Ginger Horse, one of Ugarov's early works, is a masterpiece of the Leningrad school of painting. This work is on permanent display in the 20th century art exposition in the Tretyakov Gallery. The artist manifests the traditions of the peasant genre practiced by Valentin Serov and Konstantin Korovin.

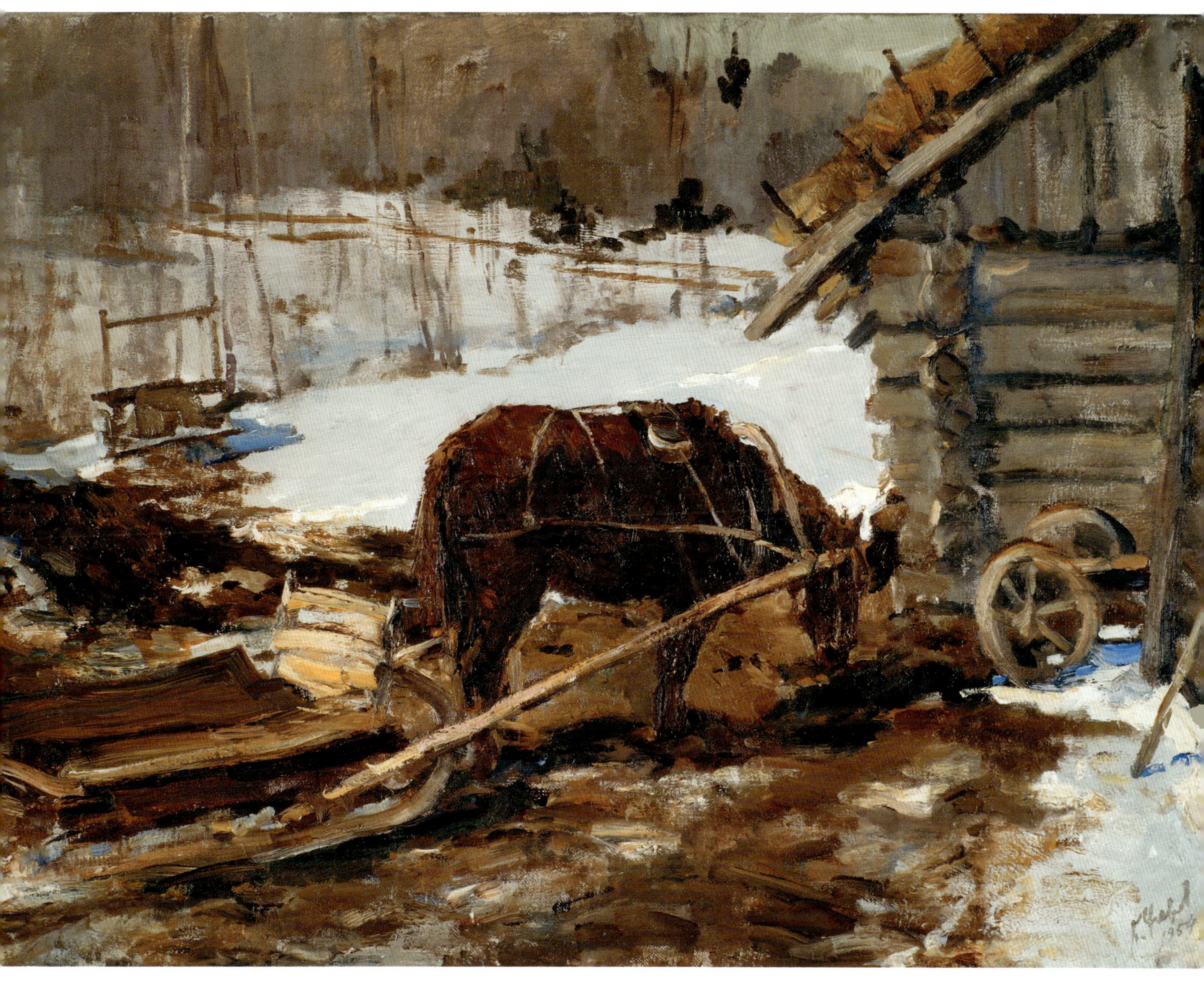

Georgi G. NISSKI

1903 – 1987

Moscow Suburbs. February. 1957
Oil on canvas. 46¾ x 75⅝ in.
(120 x 194 cm)
The State Tretyakov Gallery
Moscow, Russia

Nisski, a younger contemporary of Aleksandr Deineka, is a recognized master of the industrial landscape. The mechanical and technological symbols of the 20th century–time, speed and constant motion–are the artist's major themes. Soft fresco colors accentuated with a mere spot of crimson romanticize this landscape on the outskirts of Moscow.

Moscow Suburbs. February is one of Georgi Nisski's most popular paintings.

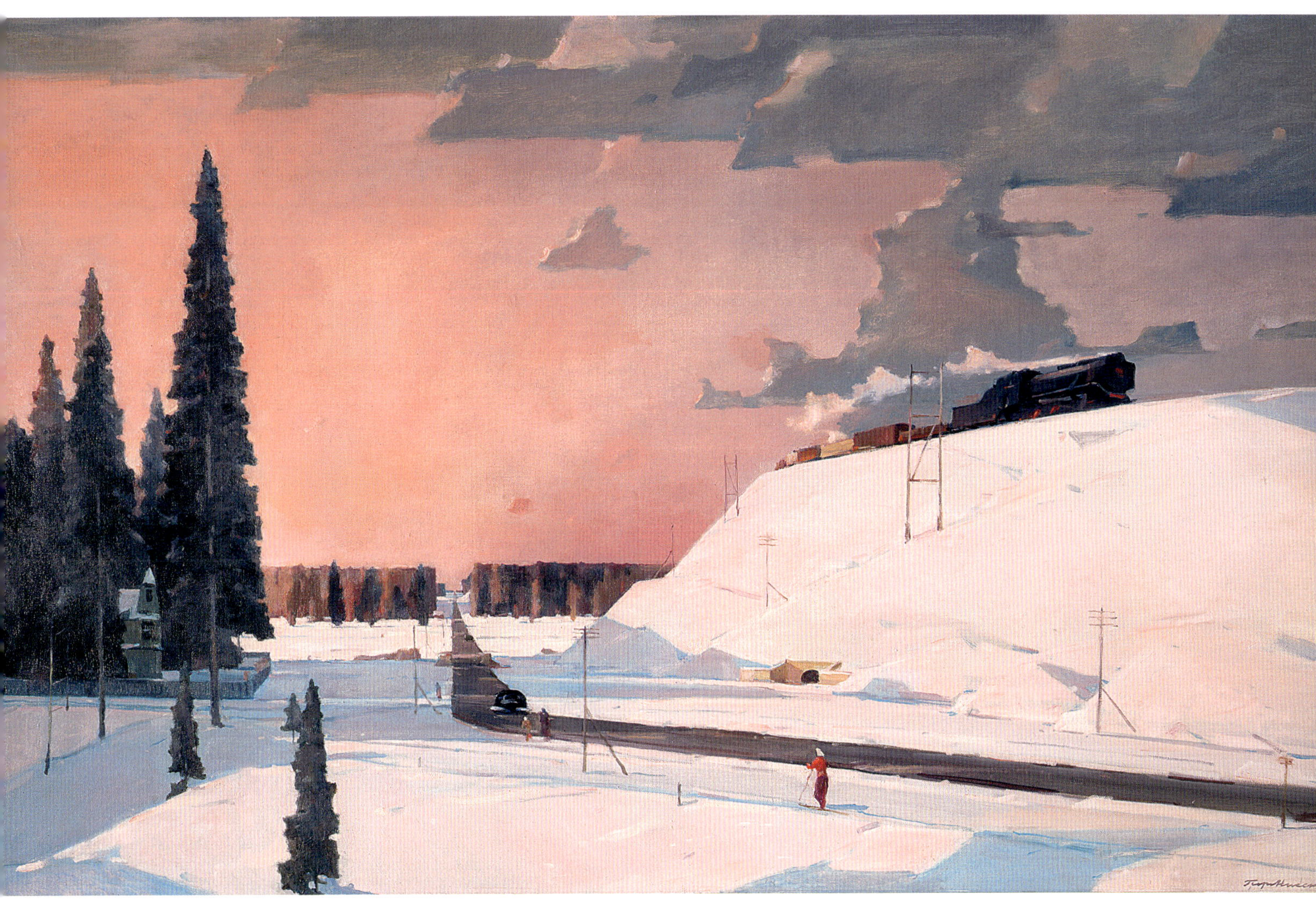

Geli M. KORZHEV

Born in 1925

Morning. 1958
Oil on canvas. 31¼ x 21¼ in.
(79 x 54 cm)
From a Private American Collection
Loan arranged by
The Museum of Russian Art
Minneapolis, Minnesota USA

The merging of the beginning day and the subject's hidden thoughts transform Morning into a metaphor for beauty and longing. The soft, pearl gray palette captures the early morning mood.

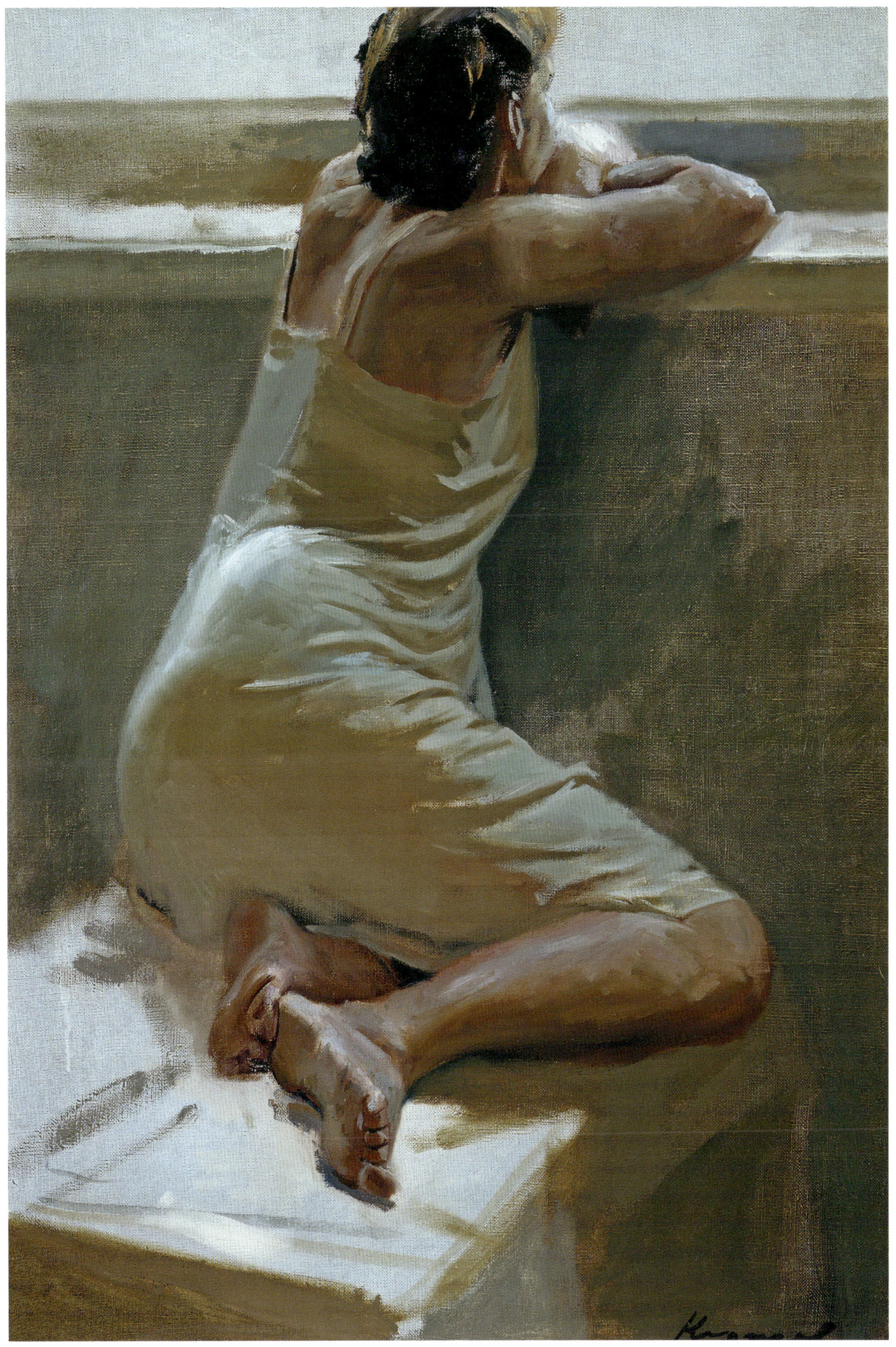

Vladimir N. GAVRILOV

1923 – 1970

A Fresh Day. 1958
Oil on canvas. 38⅝ x 69⅞ in.
(99 x 179 cm)
The State Tretyakov Gallery
Moscow, Russia

A Fresh Day is considered one of the most poetic paintings of the Soviet period. Gavrilov completed it in eight sessions, from life and in his studio. It was painted at the artists' dacha (known as the Academichka, or Academic Dacha) which is near the village of Vyshniy Volochek.

His work won recognition at once. It was awarded a gold medal at the Vienna Festival Exhibition in 1959. Even today museum visitors can share the artist's enchantment with the air, sunlight and wealth of colors.

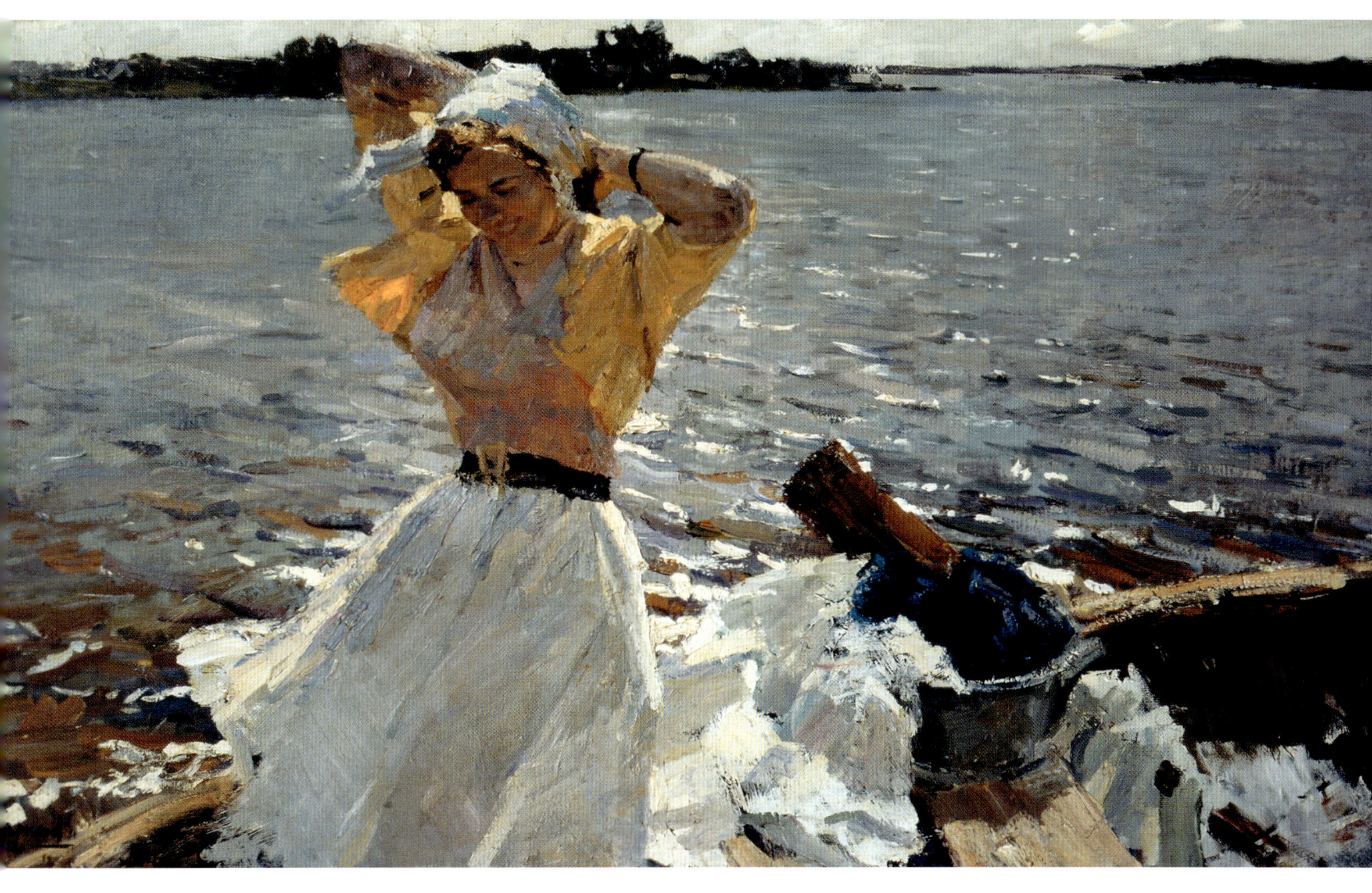

Vasily P. EFANOV

1900 – 1978

Marinka. 1959
Oil on board. 27¼ x 19½ in.
(70 x 50 cm)
The State Tretyakov Gallery
Moscow, Russia

V. Efanov is a renowned artist of the Soviet era, a brilliant master of easel portrait painters. His genre portraits always have an element of open, emotional ingenuousness. In "Marinka," the sunlight symbolizes the serenity and happiness that form a warm environment for this little girl.

The mastery and freedom of Efanov's technique places this portrait among the outstanding Russian portraits of the period.

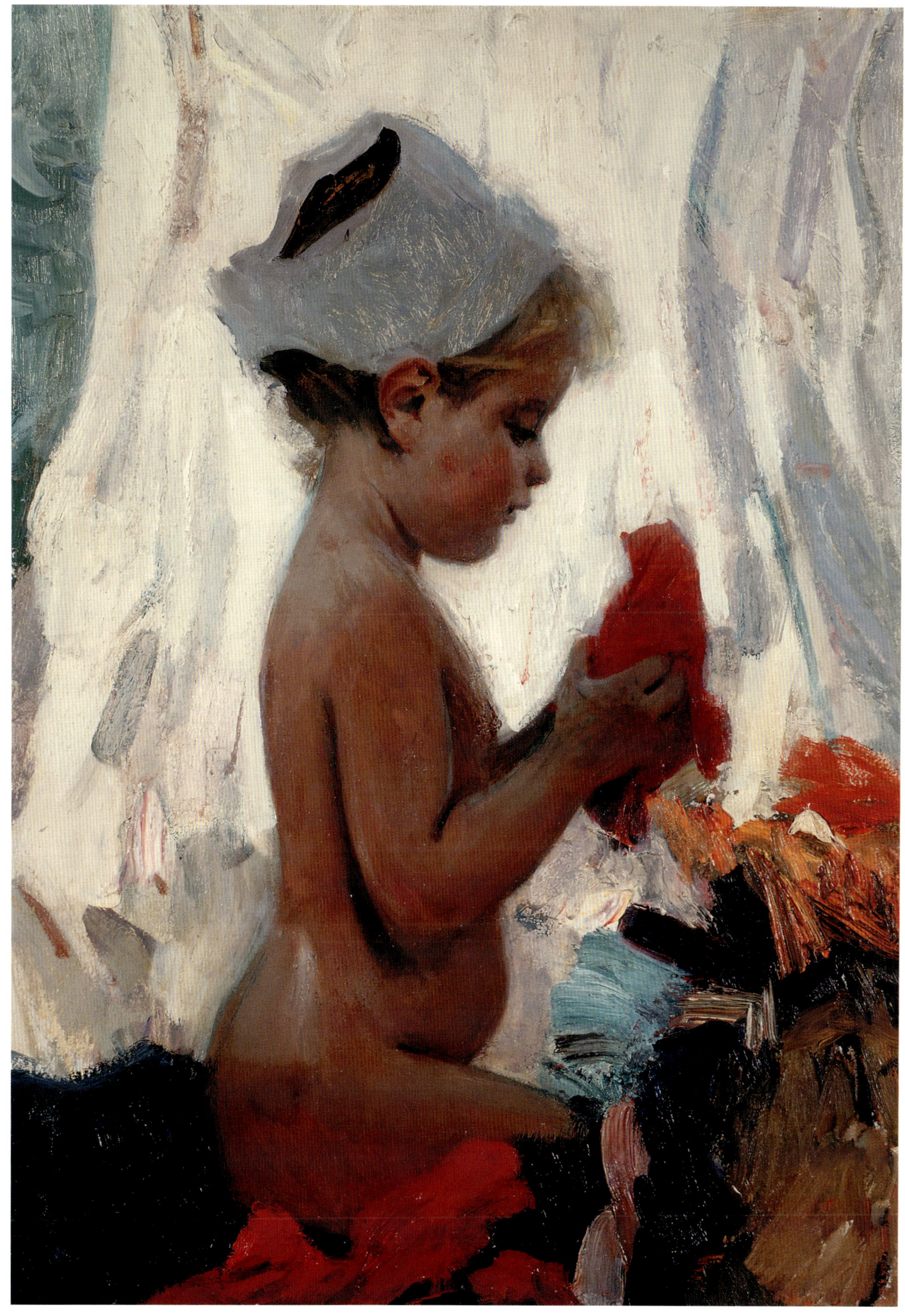

Yuri I. PIMENOV

1903 – 1977

Waiting. 1959.
Oil on board and canvas.
15⅝ x 23½ in.
(40 x 60 cm)
The State Tretyakov Gallery
Moscow, Russia

The tempo and rhythm of life and man's environment were of great interest to Pimenov when he became an artist in the 1920s. Waiting is one of the paintings in his series, "People's Belongings. Everyday Things." This painting is a unique psychological study as described by the artist: "The ordinary things that surround people are not at all inanimate.... Things can be sad or merry, they can affect a person's mood, help him or cause him pain, provoke memories and inspire wishes. A man must learn to understand things, look beyond the object itself, see its function, and what is behind it. Without this wonderful curiosity the world would be devoid of the romantic imagery of reality. Without it, things would be only monotonous inventory numbers...." Waiting is a metaphor for time.

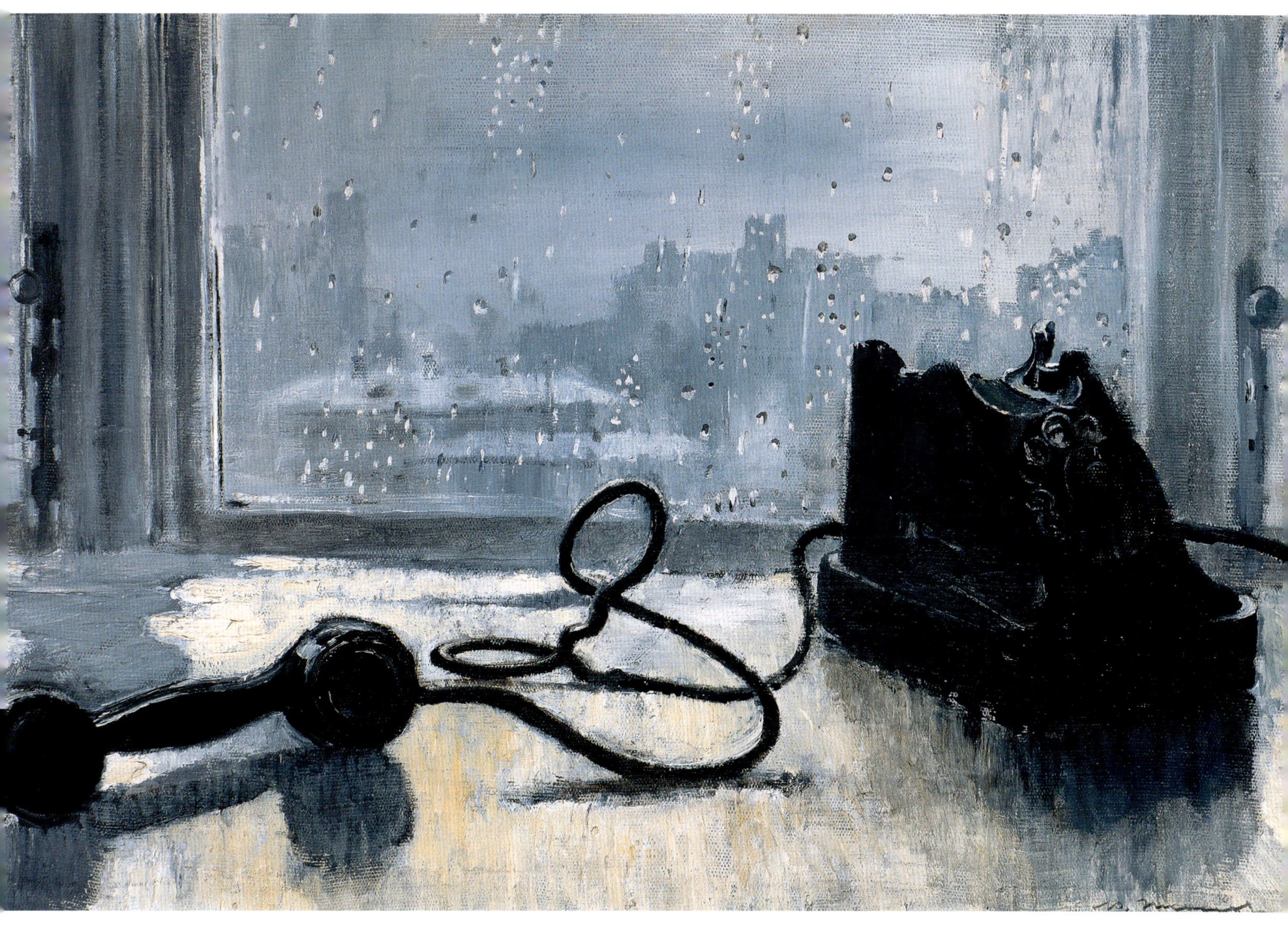

Aleksei M. GRITSAI

1914 – 1998

Blue Shadows, Msta River.
1959-1993
Oil on canvas. 18 x 31 in.
(26 x 39 cm)
From a Private American Collection
Loan arranged by
The Museum of Russian Art
Minneapolis, Minnesota USA

Aleksei Gritsai adhered closely to the classical traditions of painting Russian landscapes. The artist was always convinced that a landscape image could be created using the same rules for rendering a human image, since a landscape is an "original" portrait of a human soul.

Blue Shadows was painted by Gritsai at the Academic Dacha on the Msta River, an artists' retreat where artists gathered to paint together. Valentin Sidorov remembers a time when Gritsai worked at the Academic Dacha. "Each morning he left for the woods with his easel, umbrella, painting portfolio and painter's case in his hands and hanging from his shoulders. He would come back late at night, tired, wet, but truly delighted and impatiently enthusiastic about the following day.... It's impossible to count the studies Gritsai created there, each study showing a new side of the life that was awakening in the forest..."

(The Land of Inspiration. Published by 100th Anniversary of the Academic Dacha. Leningrad, 1986, p. 136).

A snowy riverbank, a woman taking water with a bucket from a hole in the ice; black water; and anticipation of the coming spring–all these elements make this painting poetically enchanting.

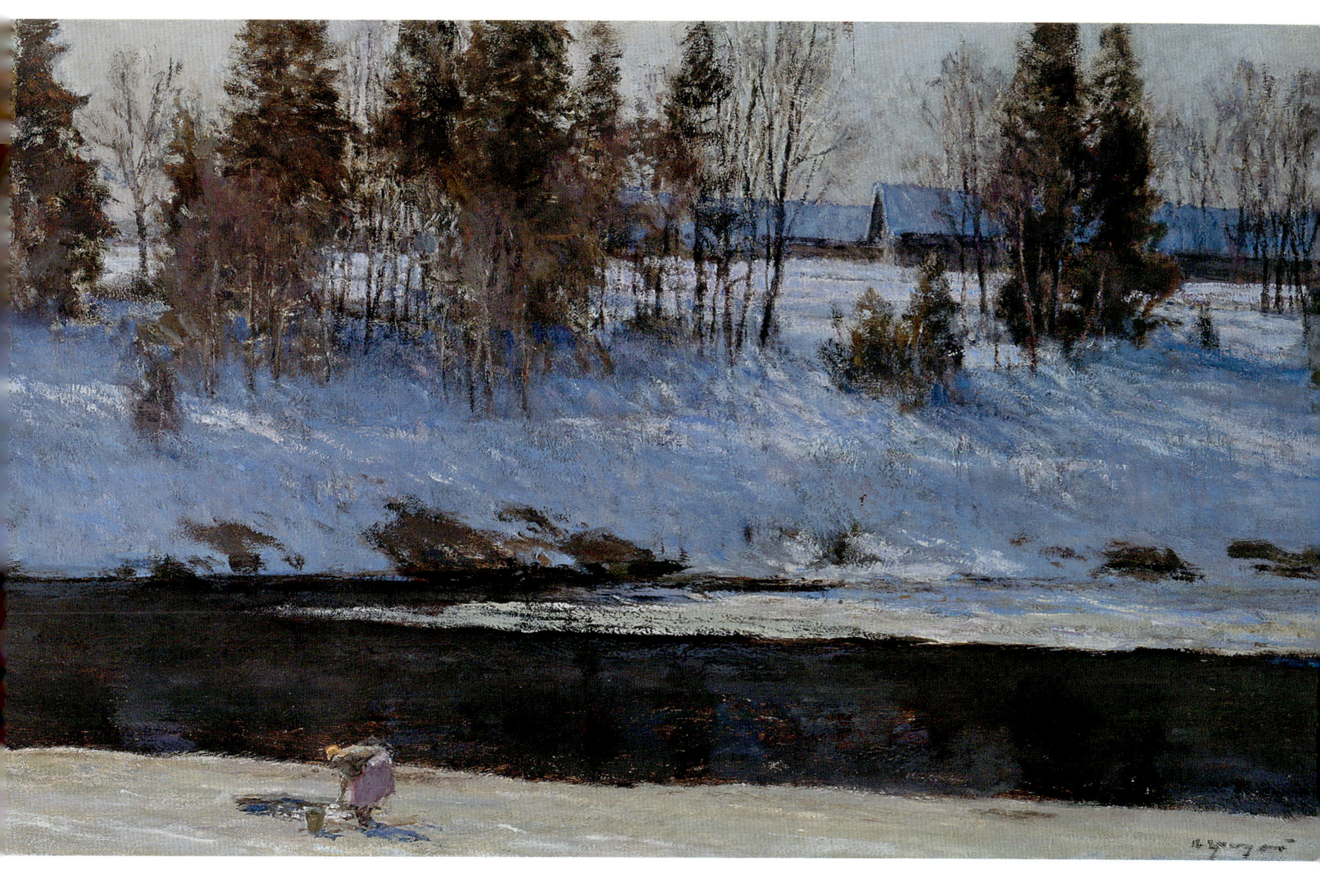

Ivan V. SOROKIN

1922 – 2003

Plesheevo Lake (August, Simak). 1960
Oil on canvas. 19 x 24 in.
(48 x 61 cm)
From a Private American Collection
Loan arranged by
The Museum of Russian Art
Minneapolis, Minnesota USA

The artist traveled extensively in the Russian north and created a series of landscapes. "I've been almost everywhere," he related in his brief biography. "I have traveled most of Russia with my paint box. One day I was walking along the shore of the White Sea, when suddenly a windstorm burst upon us and the sun appeared among the clouds lighting everything around us! I opened my case and worked for several hours. After finishing the study, I sat down on a boulder and wondered whether I had managed to depict even a glimpse of that northern evening."

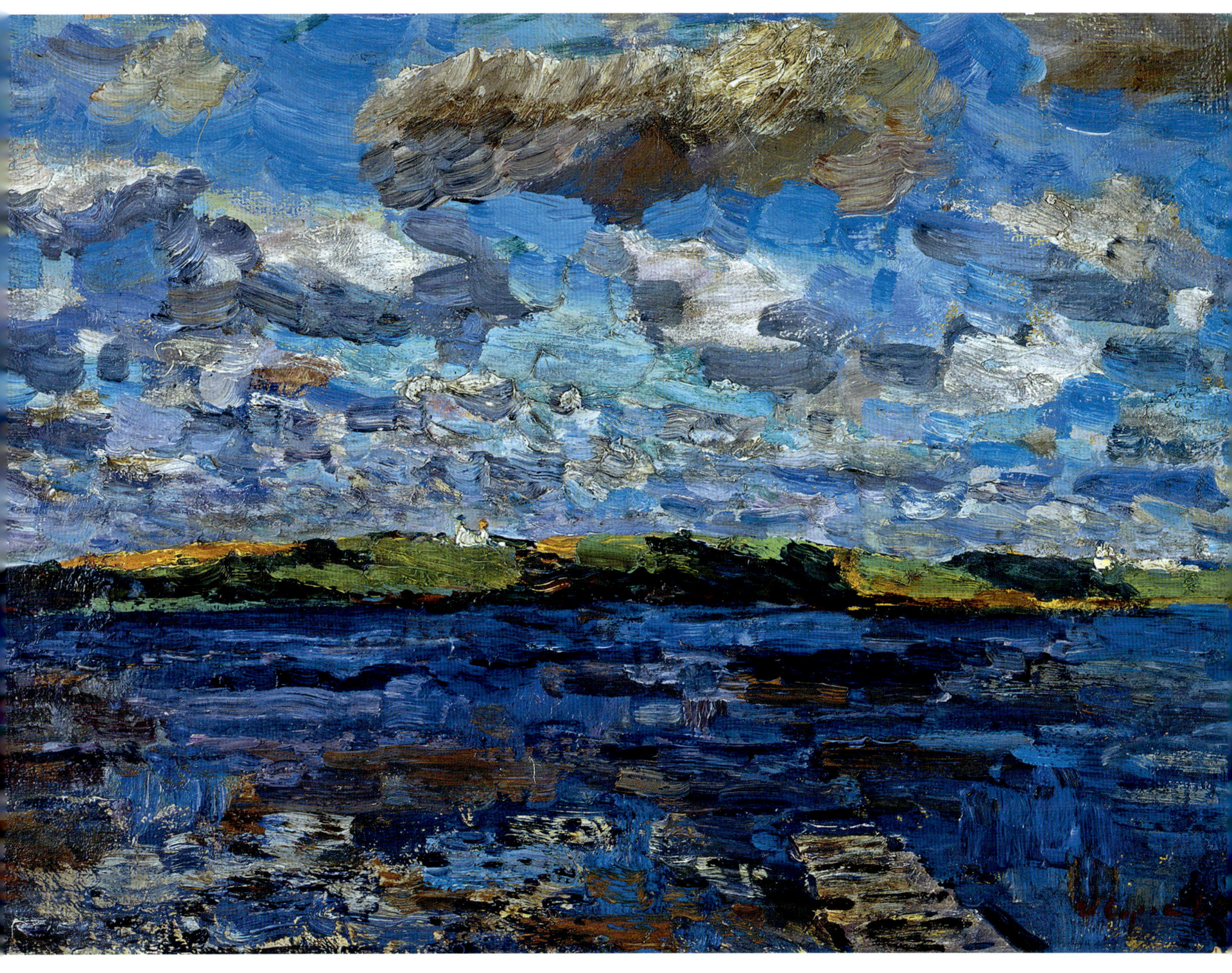

Sergei A. TUTUNOV

1925 – 1998

Winter Has Come. Childhood.
1960
Oil on canvas. 34⅜ x 45⅝ in.
(88 x 117 cm)
The State Tretyakov Gallery
Moscow, Russia

Winter light seen through a frosted window, the magical color of the season's first snow, and the changing world discovered in early childhood are the themes of Sergei Tutunov's genre, which continues the art tradition of child portraiture.

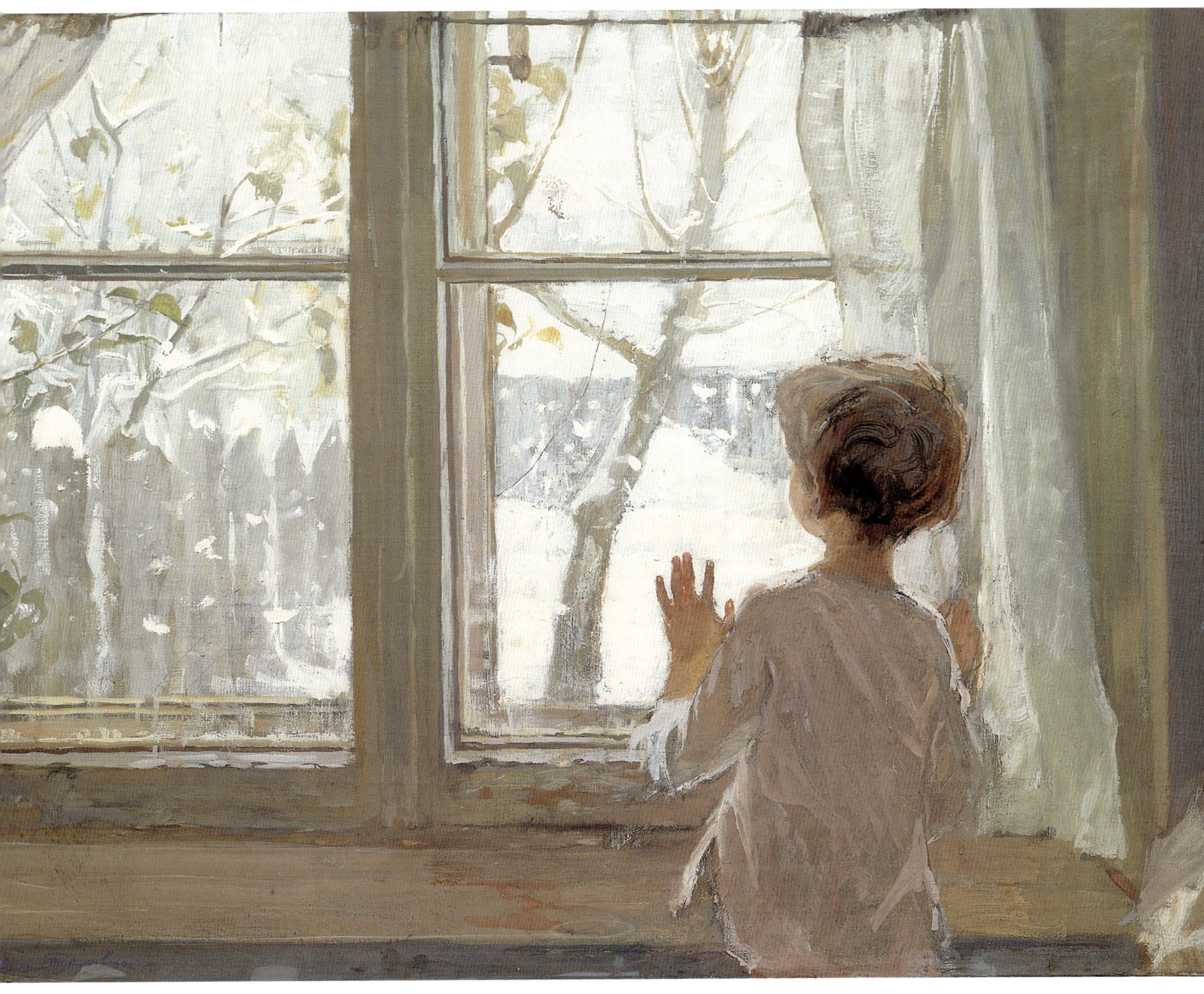

Leonid V. KABACHEK

Born in 1924

On the Way. 1961
Oil on canvas. 32¾ x 67 in.
(84 x 172 cm)
The State Tretyakov Gallery
Moscow, Russia

During his studies in the Leningrad Academy of Arts, Kabachek often participated in geological expeditions to Siberia and the Far East. In the 1950s he visited Taiga, worked in Tuva and on the Volga, and traveled across Tataria, Chuvashia, Udmurtia and Kazakhstan. Cars, planes, trains, the excitement of first impressions and the observation of almost imperceptible phenomena in everyday life–all these things shaped the artist's major themes.

On the Way is one of the paintings in what was intended to be the "driver's" series.

Anxiety and uncertainty of the "way" of a man who is no longer young and the beginning of the "way" of a girl who is open to the world and hopeful about her future: this is the psychological basis of the painting.

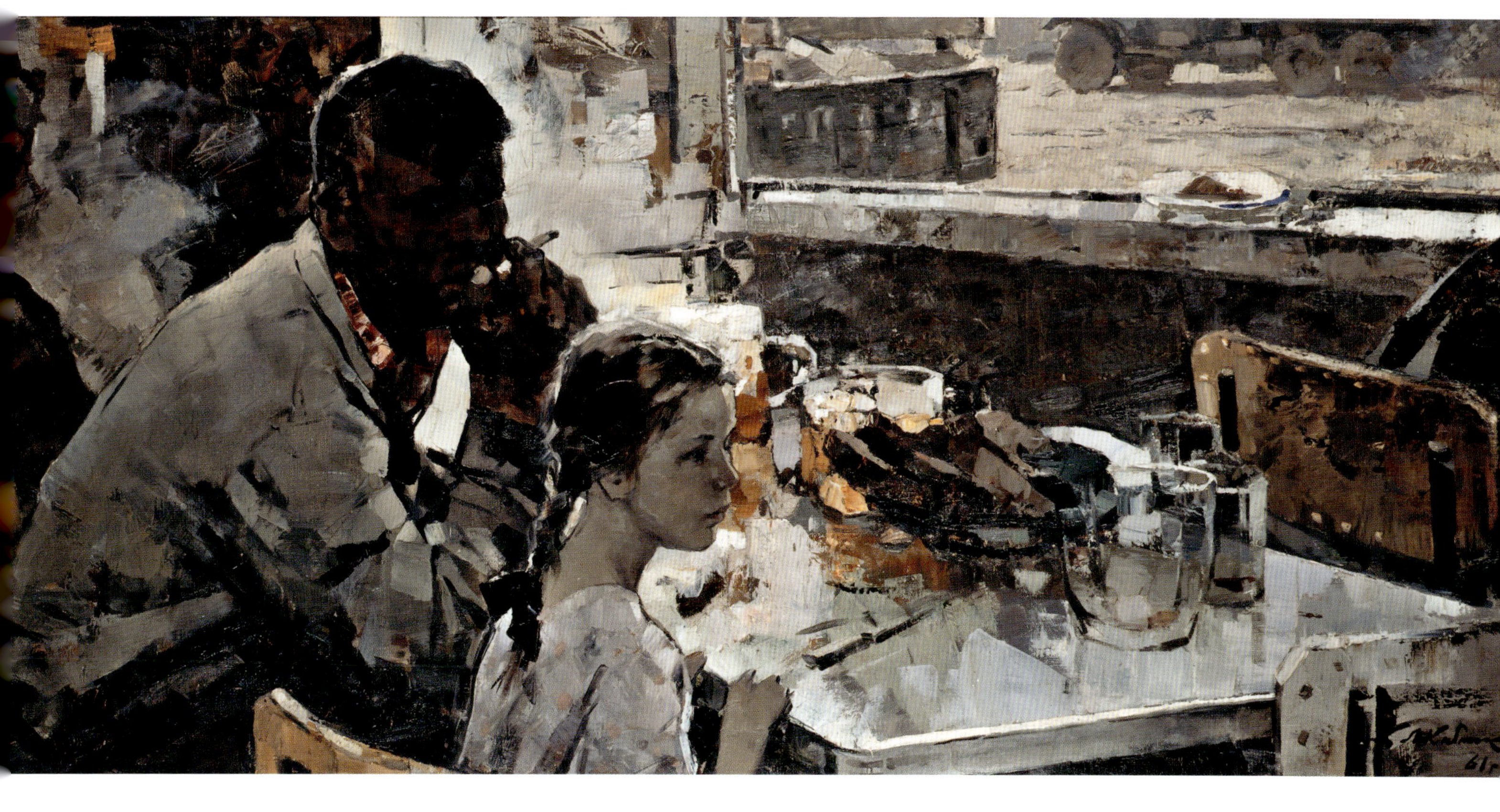

Semon A. ROTNITSKI

Born in 1915

A Holiday in Kholui. 1962
Oil on canvas. 27½ x 19½ in.
(71 x 51 cm)
From a Private American Collection
Loan arranged by
The Museum of Russian Art
Minneapolis, Minnesota USA

A graduate of the Leningrad Academy of Arts, Rotnitski worked in Kazan and St. Petersburg. The traditions of Russian Impressionism are clearly seen in this painting, in the bright winter day with the sun casting blue shadows on the snow. The artist is obviously more interested in sharing his impressions with the viewer than in depicting the festivities that are barely visible at the end of the street. "The artist's duty is to see the beauty of man and nature and to communicate that beauty to the spectator," Rotnitski observed. "As for the results, they will be evaluated by my contemporaries and judged by artists not yet born."

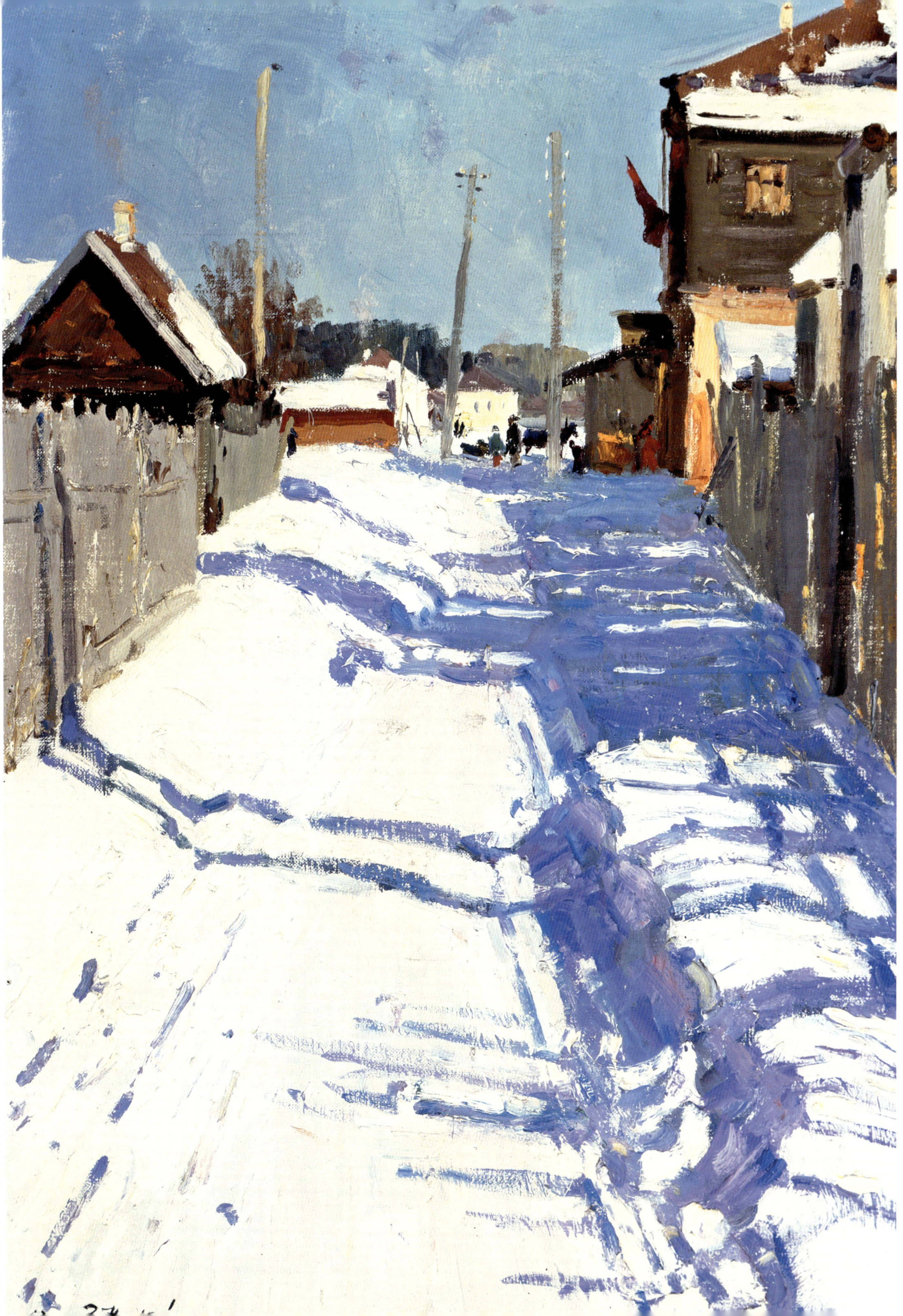

Nikolai N. BASKAKOV

Born in 1918

Milkmaids, Novella. 1962
Oil on canvas. 47 x 90¼ in.
(119 x 229 cm)
From a Private American Collection
Loan arranged by
The Museum of Russian Art
Minneapolis, Minnesota USA

In most respects, Russian artists tended to paint sedate, demure subjects. A dramatic departure is this painting of milkmaids at leisure, enjoying what must have been a hilarious joke. Baskakov, a graduate of the Leningrad Academy of Arts, painted with professionalism and skill a number of everyday situations into which he injected joy, humor, optimism and sympathy. His more serious work reflected the war years, contributing to his fame and renown.

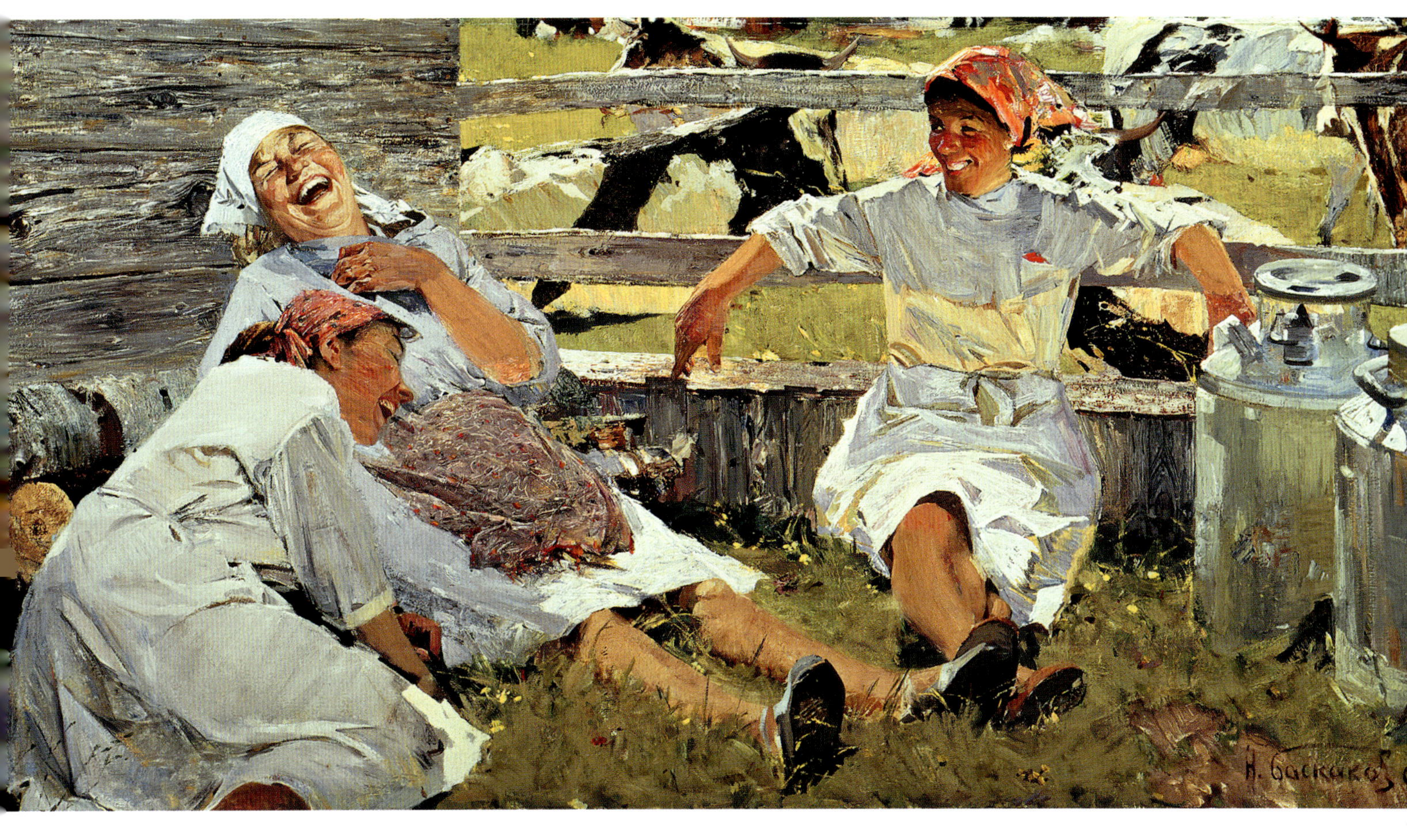
Н. Баскаков

Igor A. POPOV

1927 – 1999

Our Courtyard. 1964
Oil on canvas. 74½ x 63¼ in.
(189 x 163 cm)
From a Private American Collection
Loan arranged by
The Museum of Russian Art
Minneapolis, Minnesota USA

Igor Popov painted the courtyard of the House of Artists on Bryanskaya Street in Moscow as he viewed it from the window of his studio. Although he developed as an artist through his travels in the north, where age-old traditions had merged with the modern way of life, he returned to Moscow, and by the late 1960s he was depicting the real beauty of daily life in the city. The artist saw love, birth and death–the biblical rotation of life–in an ordinary Moscow courtyard.

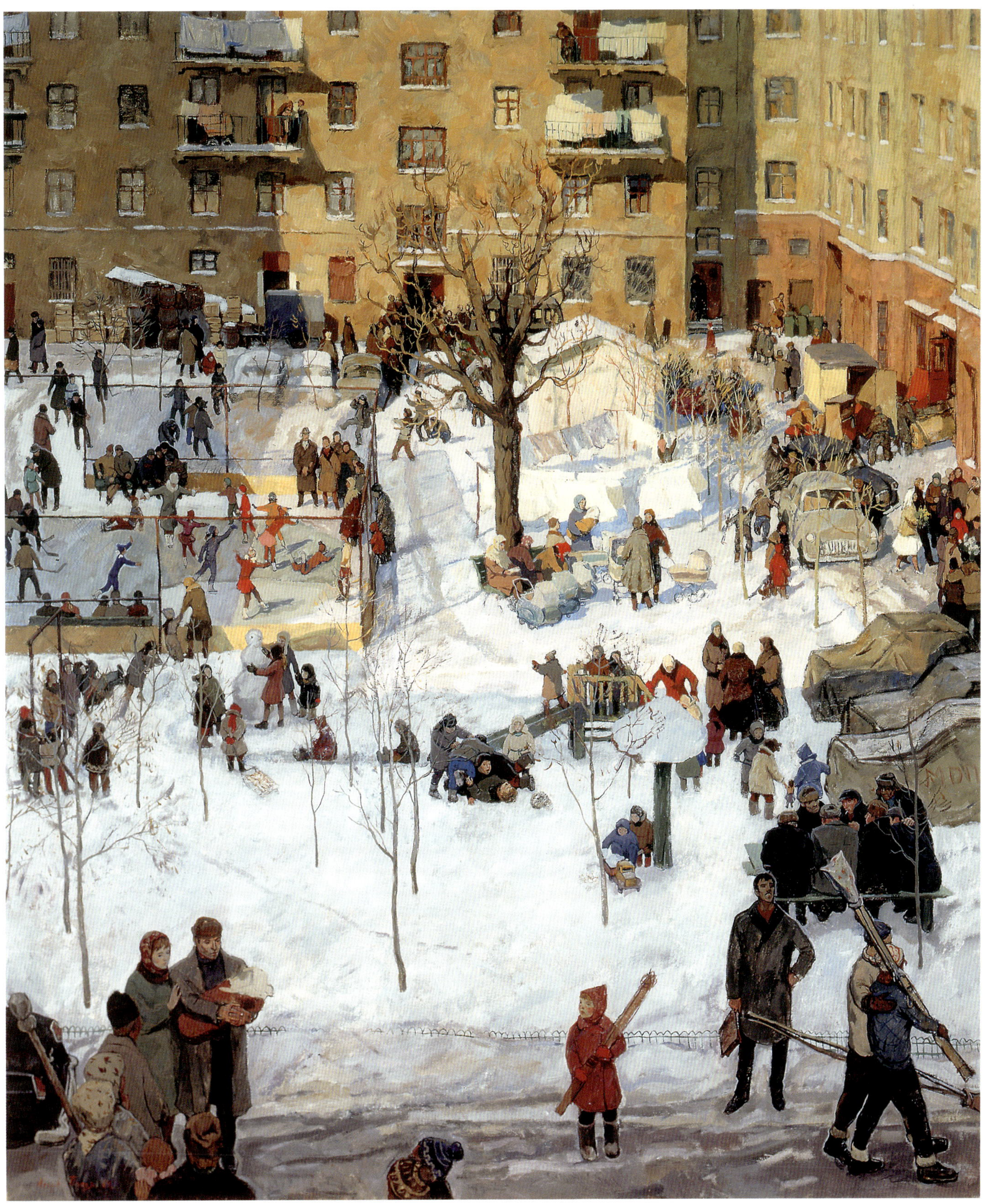

Eduard G. BRAGOVSKY

Born in 1923

Logging on the Vetluga River. 1964
Oil on canvas. 59 x 79 in.
(150 x 201 cm)
From a Private American Collection
Loan arranged by
The Museum of Russian Art
Minneapolis, Minnesota USA

"Vetluga is a Volga River tributary," the artist has noted. "We were boating from the city of Nizhniy when logs were being rafted along the Vetluga River. I am still impressed by the steep riverbanks that appeared almost red in the distance. I always base my palette on a single color that acts as a tuning fork. An impressionistic 'color' serves as a hollow in the space. I create colors in and around the space...."

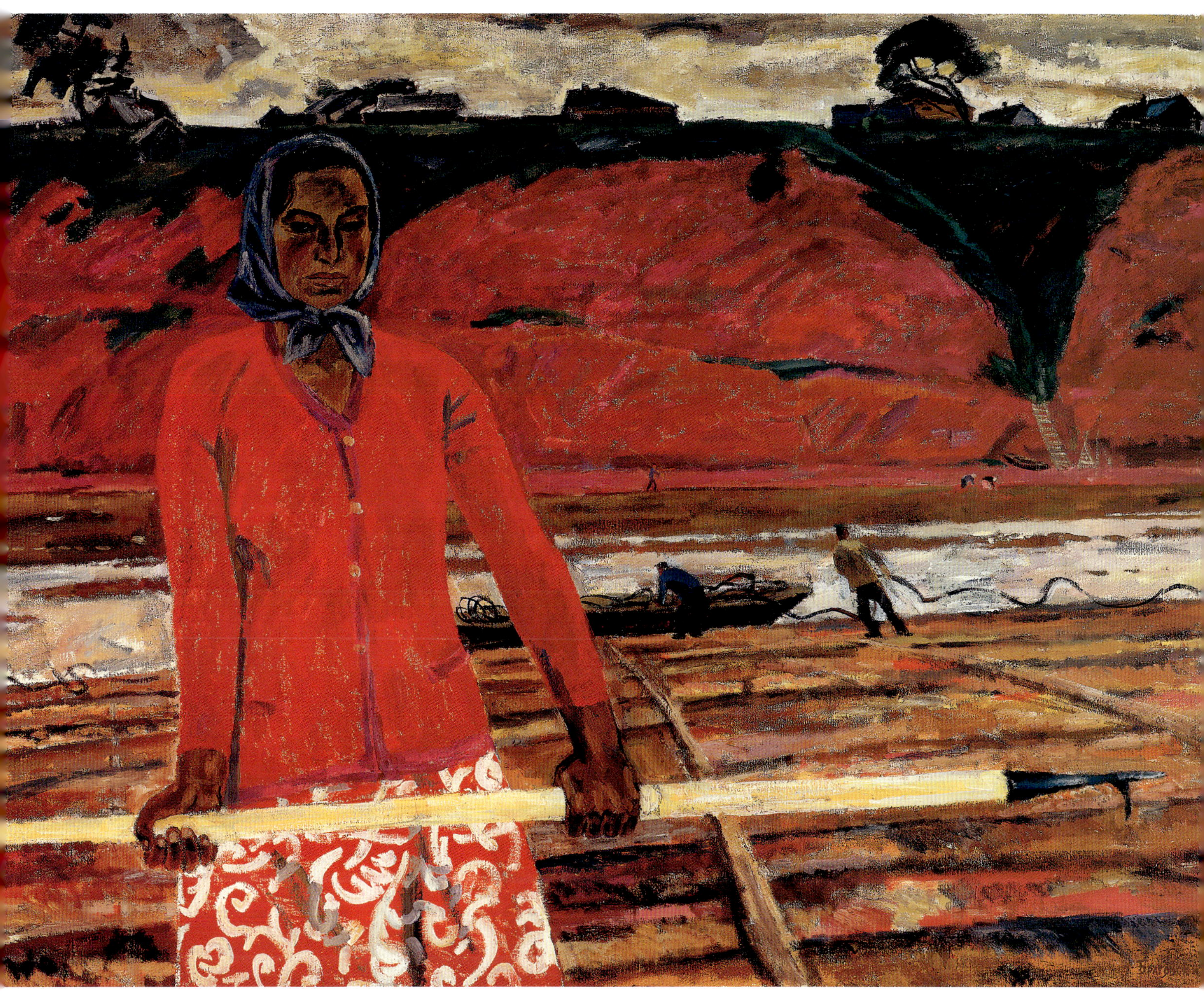

Nikolai E. TIMKOV

1912 – 1993

Winter Laundry Line. 1965
Oil on board. 20⅜ x 28¾ in.
(51,7 x 73 cm)
From a Private American Collection
Loan arranged by
The Museum of Russian Art
Minneapolis, Minnesota USA

Lauded as one of the great landscape painters of the second half of the 20th century, Timkov also was one of the St. Petersburg painters who memorialized Russian provinces, their historic towns and villages. Due to the fact that he was trained in the academic traditions of Russian realism at the Academy of Arts, he developed his own unique style characterized by impressionistic brushwork and fresh compositions. Expressive and panoramic, his landscapes reveal the artist's careful observations of nature's seasonal changes and his love of the earth. He is perhaps best known for his snow scenes. Timkov painted mostly from life and he was always interested in solving various color challenges. Here a viewer can see that the artist is interested in the way the colored clothing can be shown on a background of white snow. Timkov cultivated nature as the apotheosis of beauty, and humans are an integral part of nature.

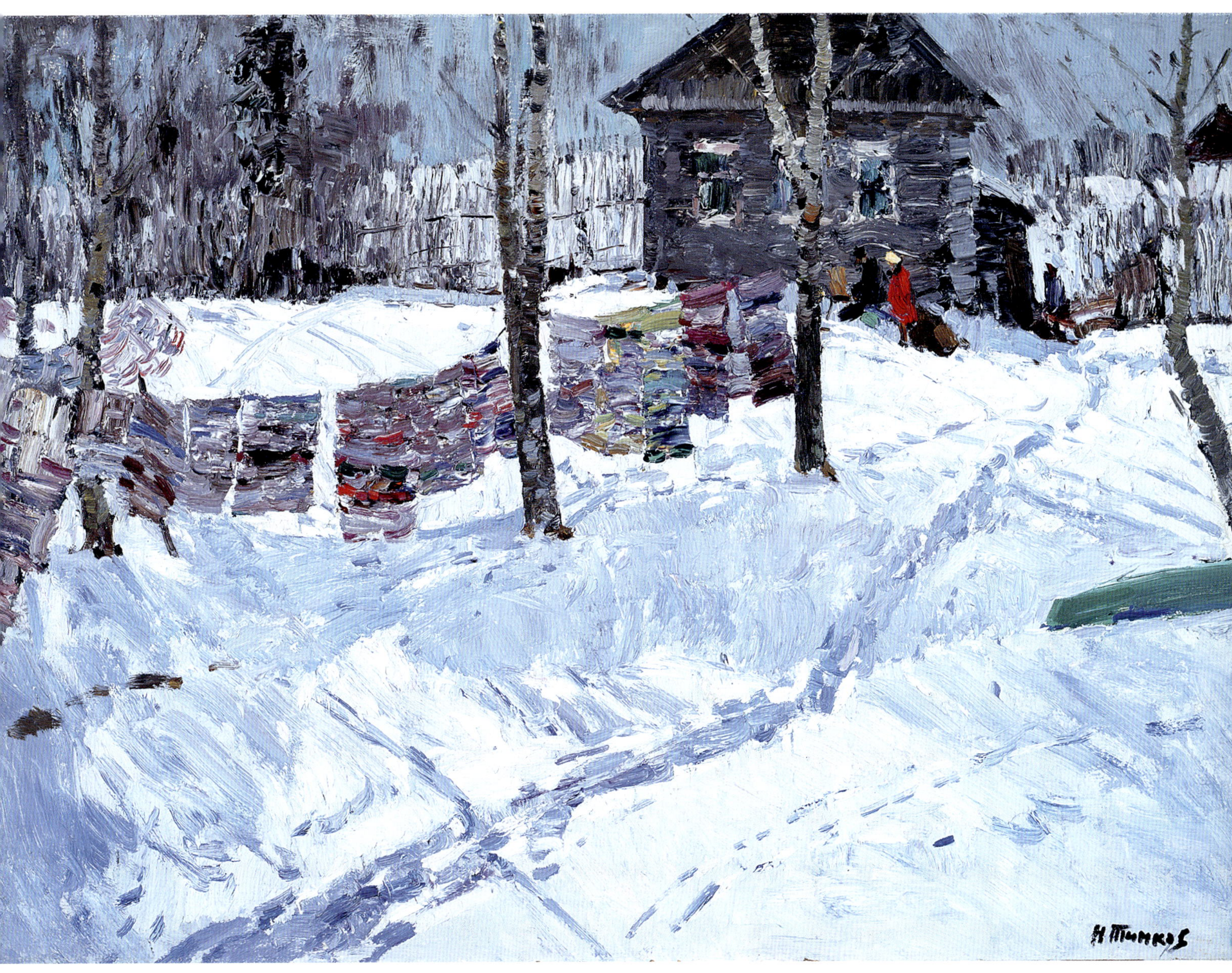
Н Тимков

Tair T. SALAKHOV

Born in 1928

Aidan. 1967
Oil on canvas. 43 x 31¼ in.
(110 x 80 cm)
The State Tretyakov Gallery
Moscow, Russia

Aidan T. Salakhova, the artist's daughter, is depicted in the painting.

Among the rare portraits of children painted during the second half of the 20th century on exhibit in The State Tretyakov Gallery, Aidan is very significant. Capturing the girl's subtlety, tenderness and personality is achieved by laconic and minimal artistic means consistent with this time.

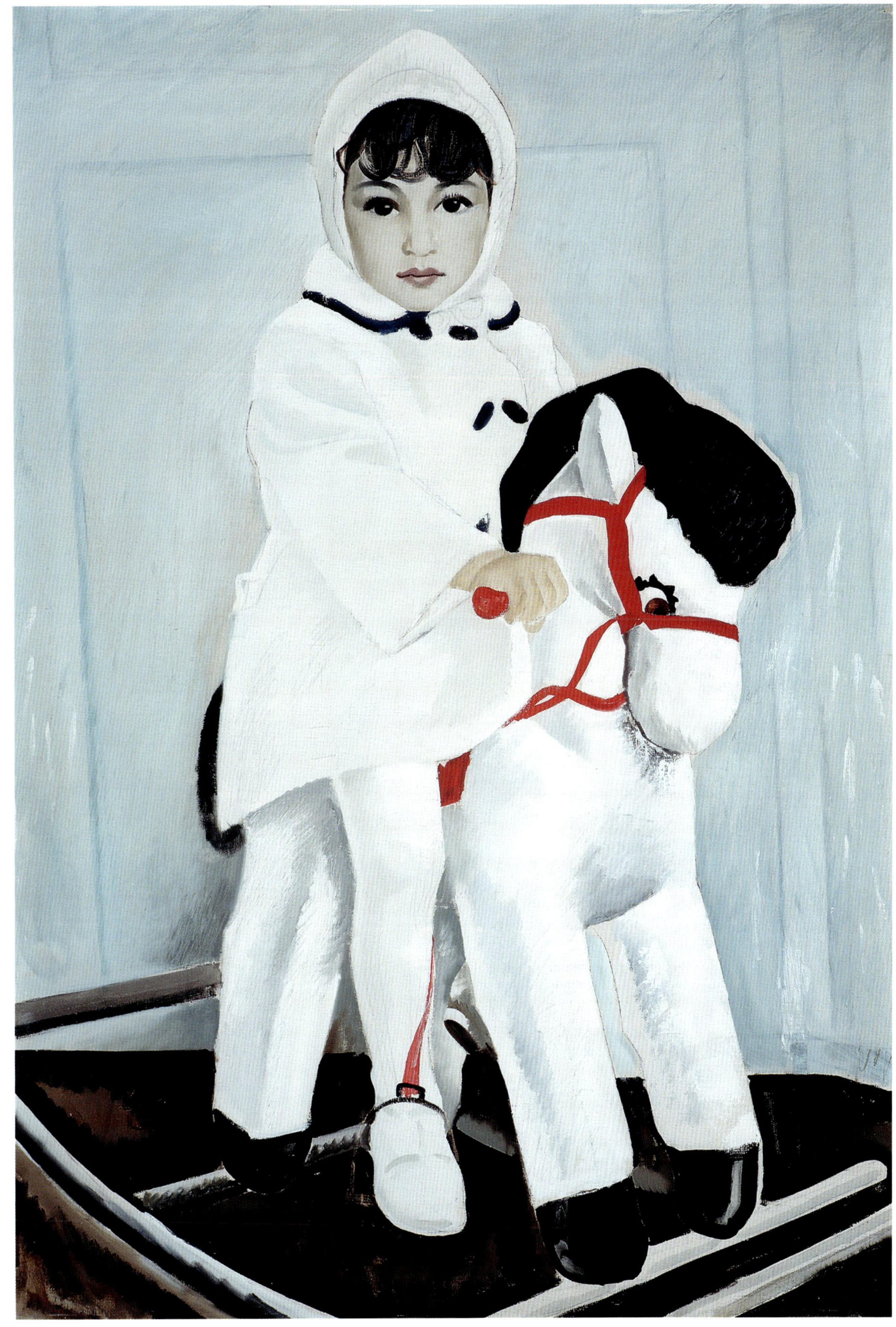

Viktor E. POPKOV

1932 – 1974

Family in July. 1969
Oil on canvas. 59 x 74 in.
(150 x 188 cm)
The Museum of Russian Art
Minneapolis, Minnesota USA

Popkov's art is remarkable for its deep appreciation of all aspects of life. In his Family in July the artist has painted the basic element of society, the nucleus of human existence in the harmony of family life. The painting is also metaphoric: three characters aloft in the universe are the symbol of eternal life.

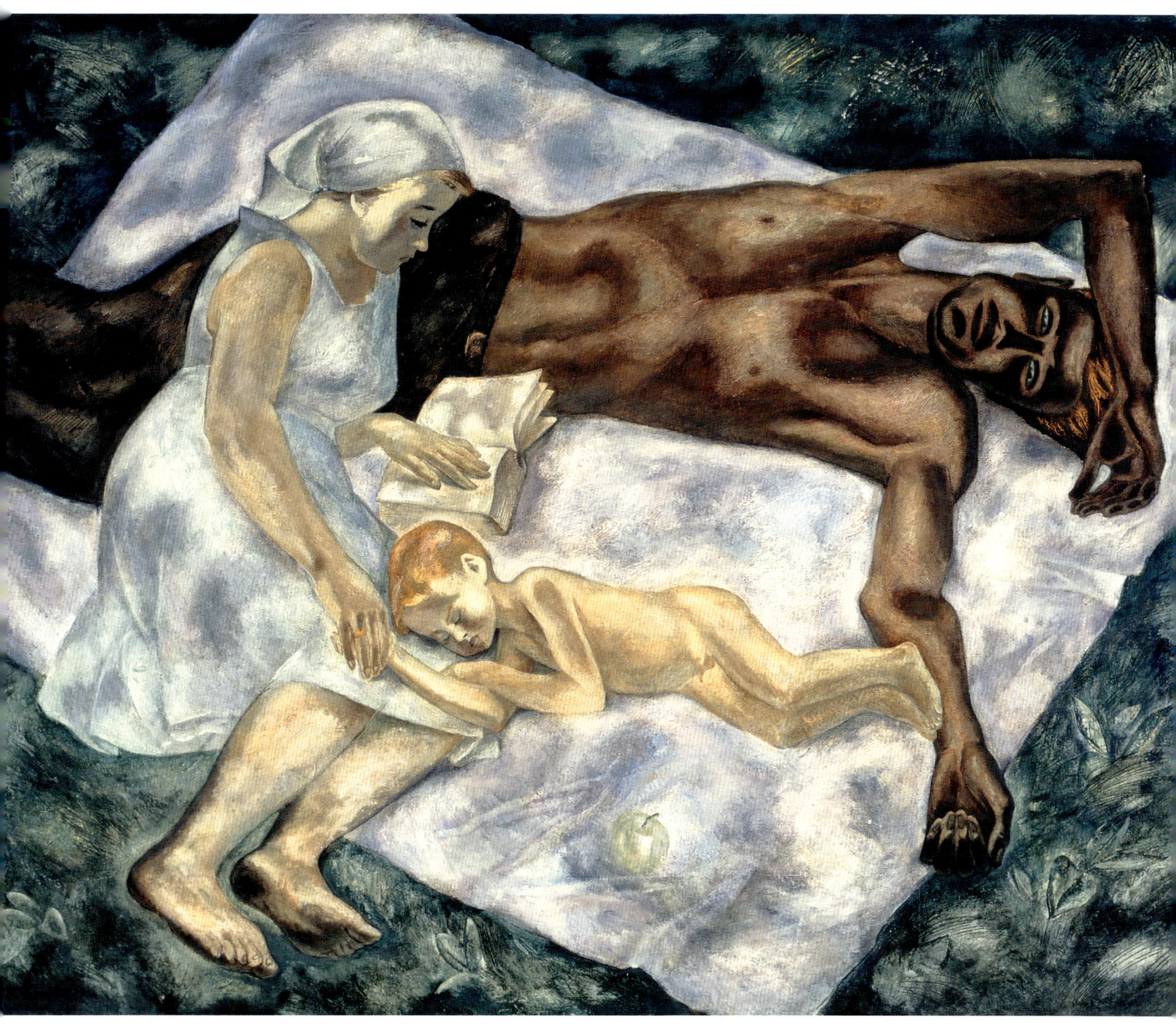

Viktor E. POPKOV

1932 – 1974

Remembering. Widows. 1969
Oil on canvas. 62½ x 87⅜ in.
(160 x 224 cm)
The State Tretyakov Gallery
Moscow, Russia

Remembering. Widows is one of the artist's series of works that he painted after traveling in the northern part of Russia. Popkov depicted a Russian izba (a log house) where old women gathered to exchange stories of their youth, the Great War, and the death of their husbands, which doomed them to loneliness.

The metaphoric style of Popkov's painting seems to absorb the poignant and lyrical flavor of Russian folklore. These village widows symbolize eternal fidelity, femininity and their generation's collective memory of World War II.

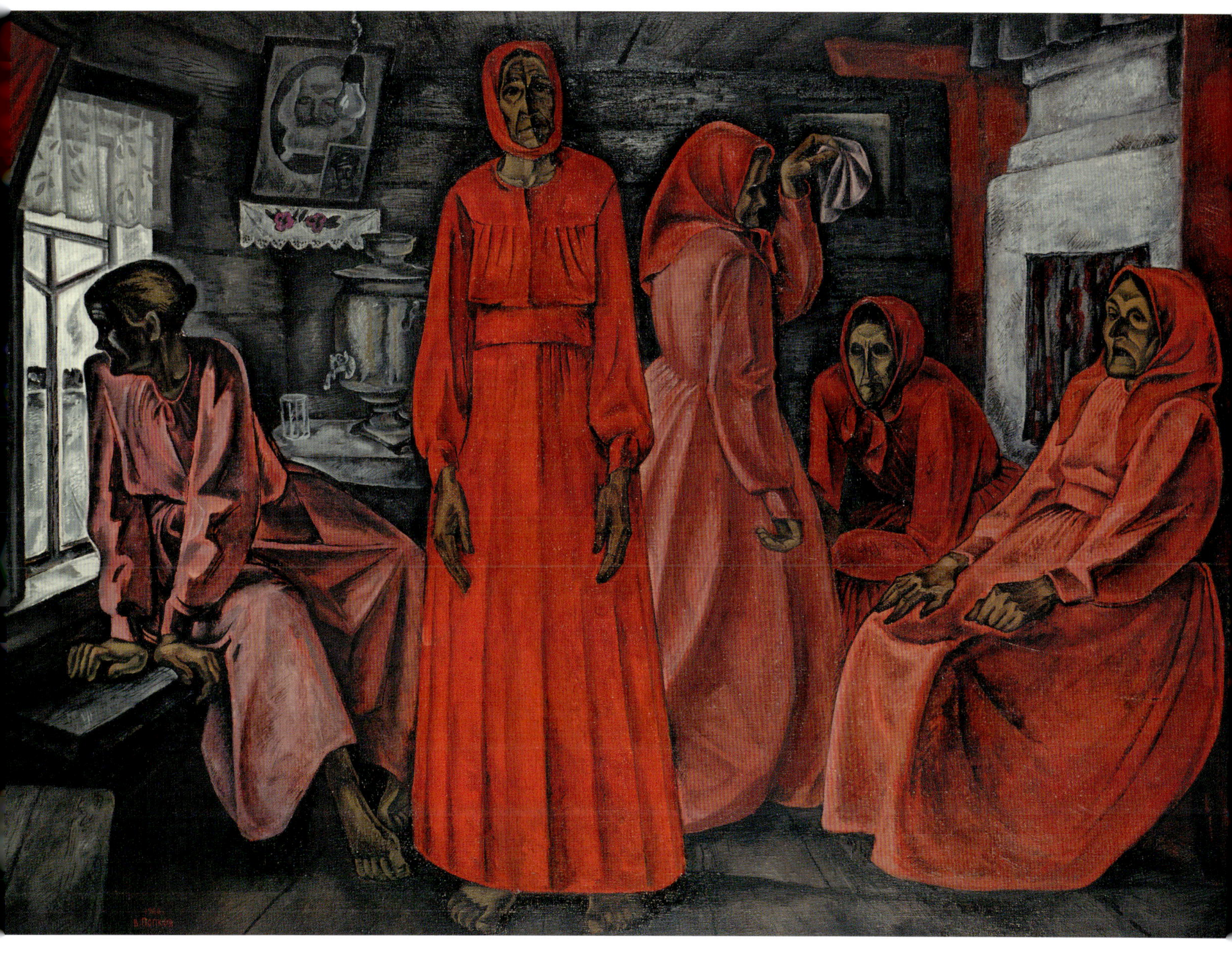

Boris S. UGAROV

1922 – 1991

Tanya's Portrait. 1971
Oil on canvas. 49½ x 32 in.
(127 x 82 cm)
The State Tretyakov Gallery
Moscow, Russia

Tatyana B. Ugarova, the artist's daughter, sat for this portrait.

The compositions of Boris Ugarov, who was born in Leningrad, are often dynamic in their impact, with stark contrasts between black and white and effected in quick, spare brushstrokes.

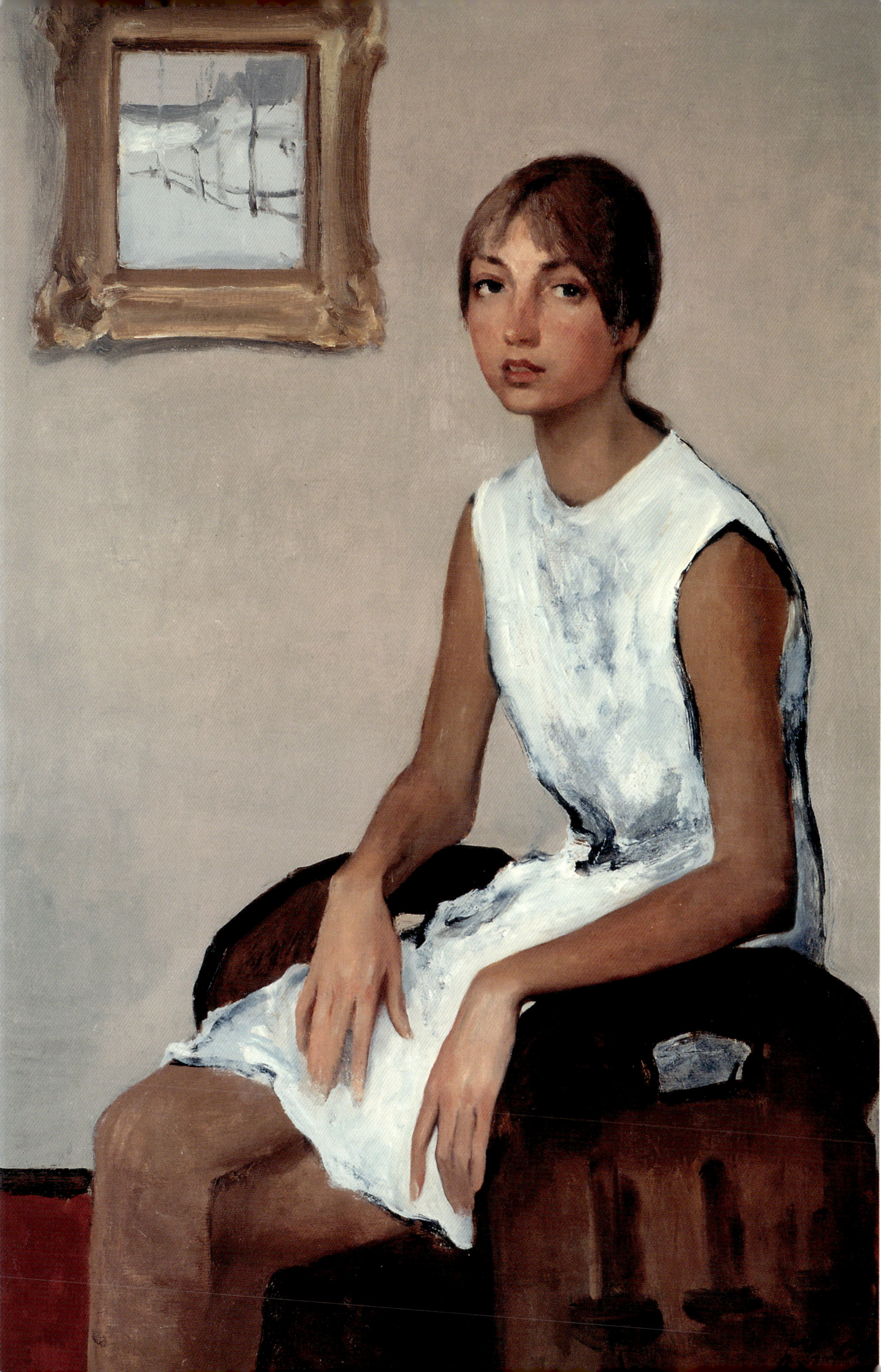

Vladimir F. STOZHAROV

1926 – 1973

Novgorod. Yaroslav Monastery. 1972
Oil on canvas. 39¼ x 55 in.
(100 x 140 cm)
From a Private American Collection
Loan arranged by
The Museum of Russian Art
Minneapolis, Minnesota USA

Stozharov's artist friends remember how he energized his work: "...Stozharov traveled about all northern Russia and...Siberia... He used to visit the places he loved and where he could re-discover himself... He would go deep into the region where primordial Russia originated and still existed. His art strengthened, his own manner of painting became visible in his works, and his multicolor palette appeared...."

"Volodya Stozharov was struck by northern nights," according to artist Ivan Sorokin. The northern night theme enchanted him...Volodya revealed his own character; his works became colorful and quite different from our mid-country landscape...."

(V. Stozharov. Moscow, 1977, p. 60, p. 50)

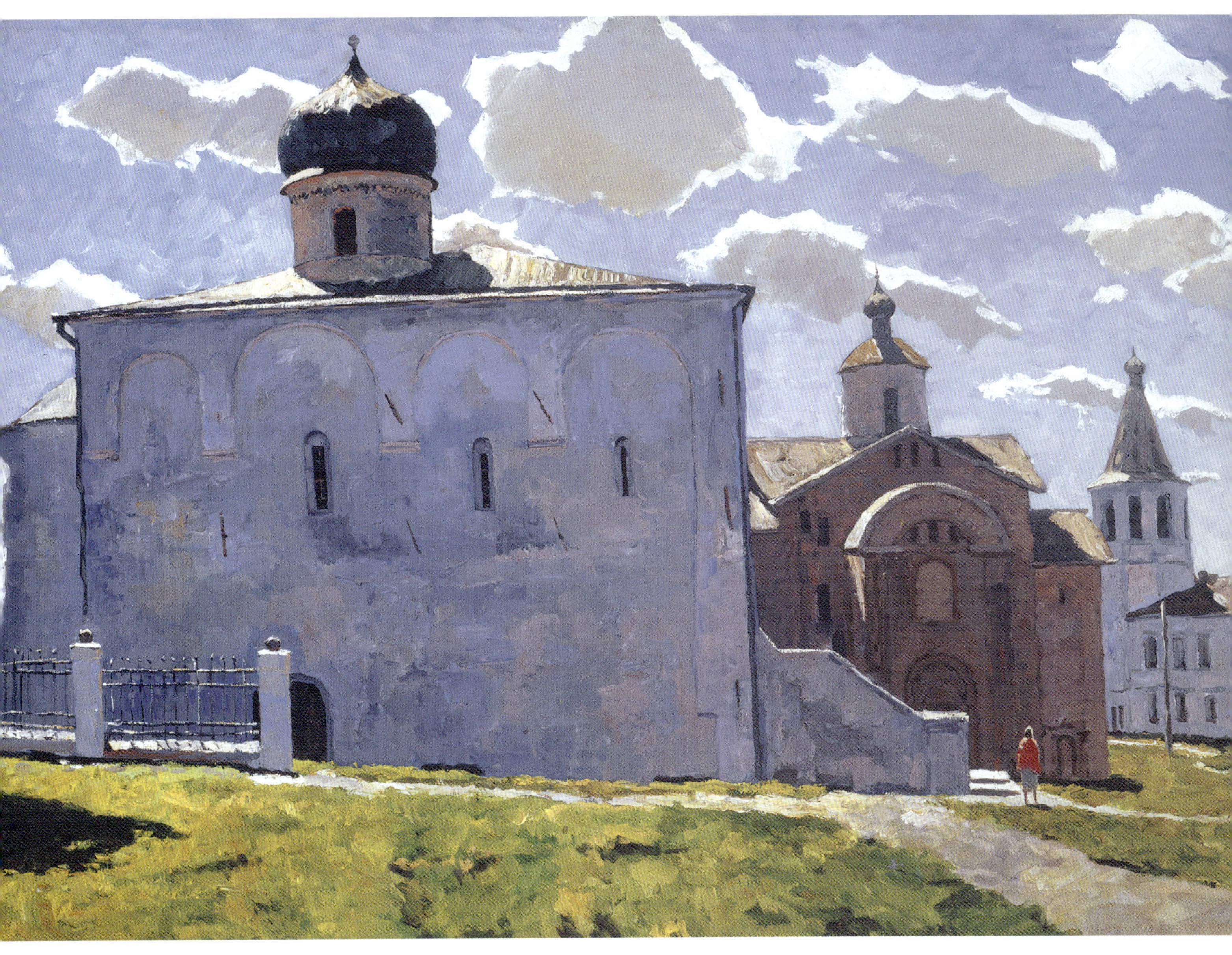

Vasili K. NECHITAILO

1915 – 1980

Nude. Masha. 1976
Oil on canvas. 59½ x 63¼ in
(151 x 120 cm)
From a Private American Collection
Loan arranged by
The Museum of Russian Art
Minneapolis, Minnesota USA

Maria Vladimirovna Savchenkova, the artist's wife, is the subject of this painting.

Xenia Nechitailo, the artist's daughter, has many memories of her father. "In his later years, my father somewhat unexpectedly 'clarified' his palette. A purely impressionistic color technique became characteristic of his later works. As soon as my father arrived in the Kuban region where he was born, his car became his place of residence, its trunk serving as his painting case. Father traveled about Kuban for weeks, constantly painting studies under the hot and dazzling sun...."

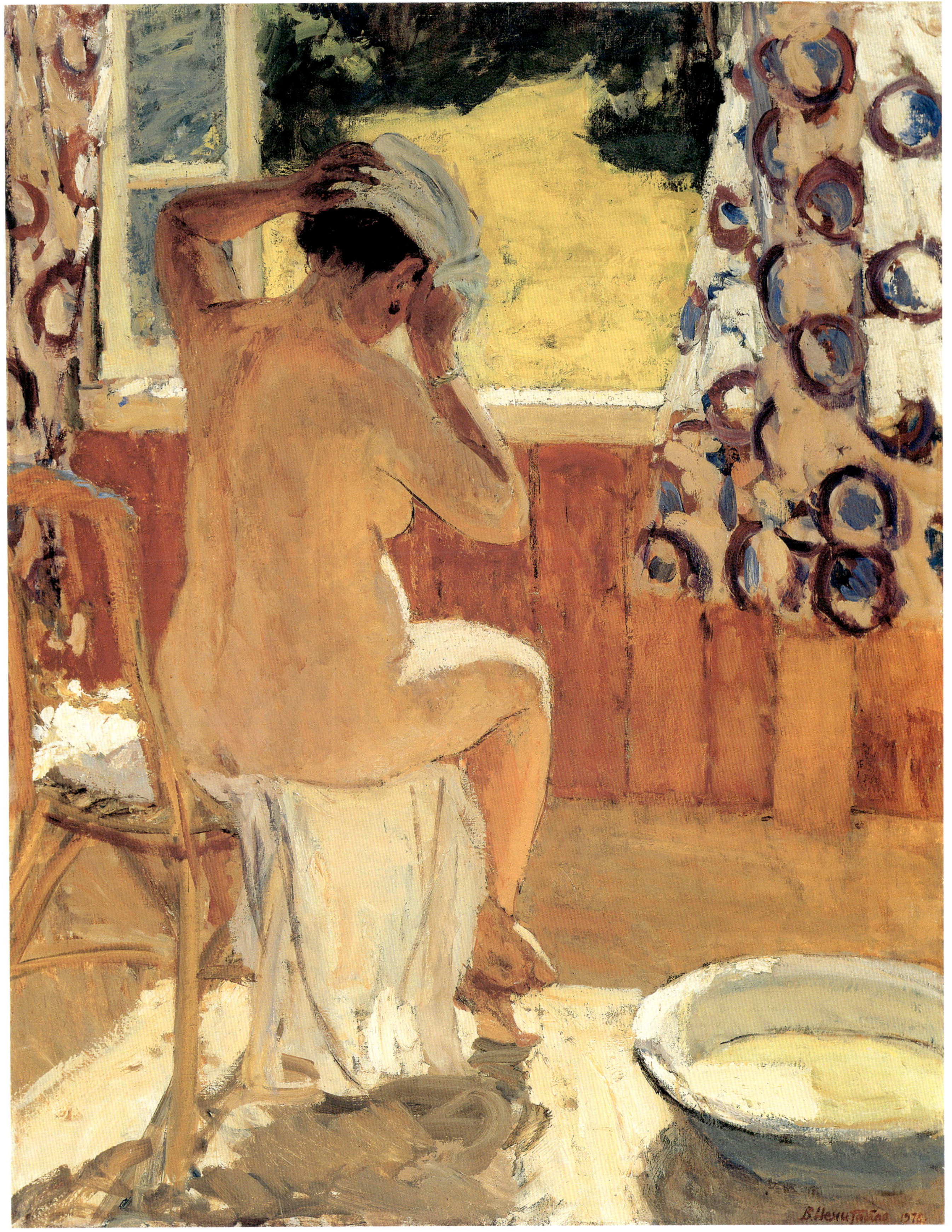

Dmitri D. ZHILINSKI

Born in 1927

Young Family. 1980
Oil on wood. 23½ x 17½ in.
(60 x 45 cm)
The State Tretyakov Gallery
Moscow, Russia

Related to Valentin Serov and Vladimir Favorski, Dmitri Zhilinski is often singled out among the post-war generation of artists. His orientation toward the "museum" style, his use of symbols and his mastery of Northern European Renaissance techniques reveal his picturesque world, a universe of beautiful people. His characterizations of man's inherent loneliness, his discord with himself and in his relationships, are in contrast with the beauty and harmony of the surrounding world.

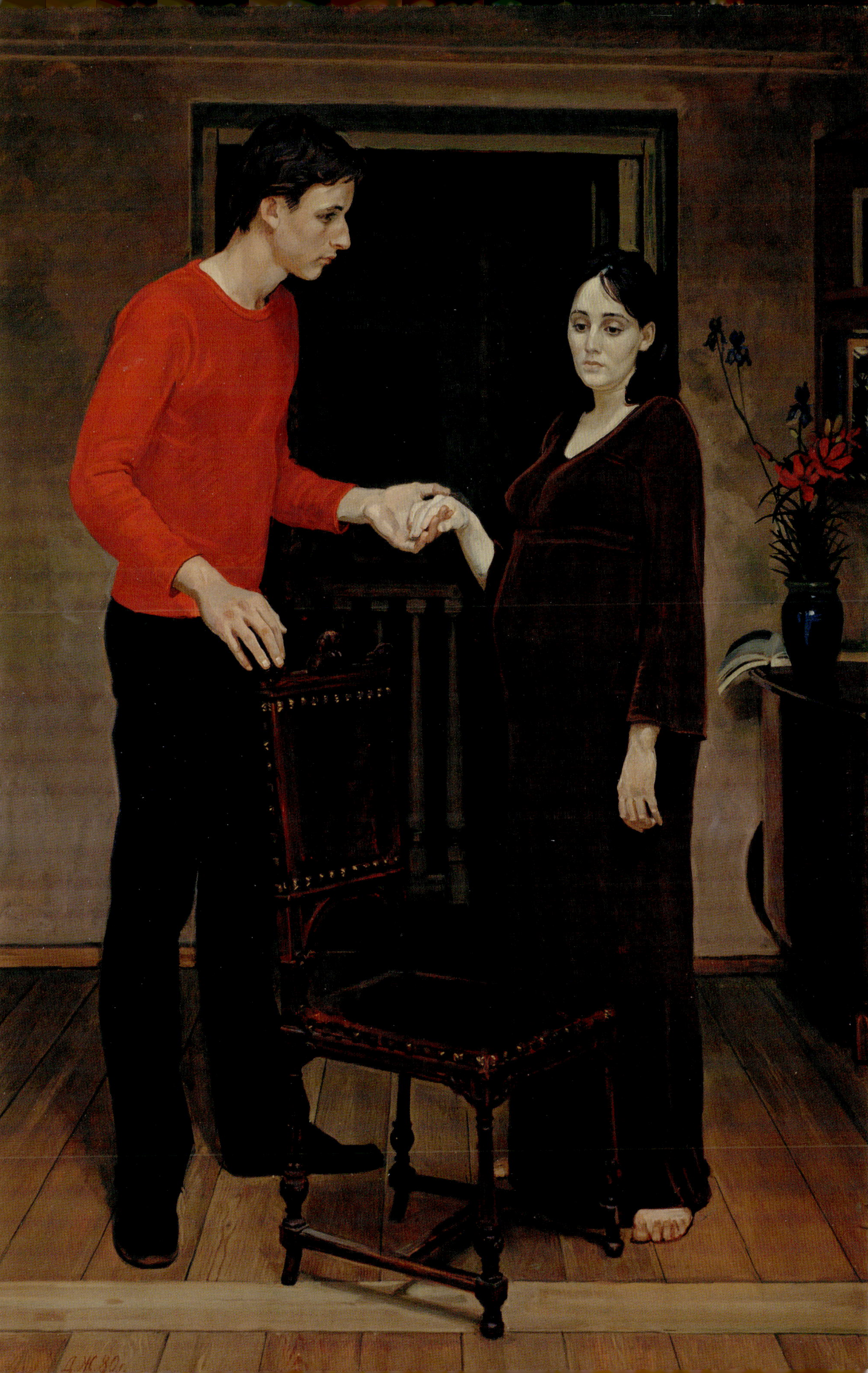

Geli M. KORZHEV

Born in 1925

Marusya. 1983-1989
Oil on canvas. 37¾ x 89¼ in.
(99 x 226,7 cm)
From a Private American Collection
Loan arranged by
The Museum of Russian Art
Minneapolis, Minnesota USA

In the 1920s, when the artist was a child, Marusya was his neighbor in a large communal flat where many families lived in 12 rooms. As did many of her contemporaries, Marusya worked at a factory, and as part of her "uniform," wore a red headscarf and heavy work boots. A true masterpiece, Marusya combines the element of one of art's oldest traditions–a beautiful sleeping nude–with realistic details that reflect the Soviet era.

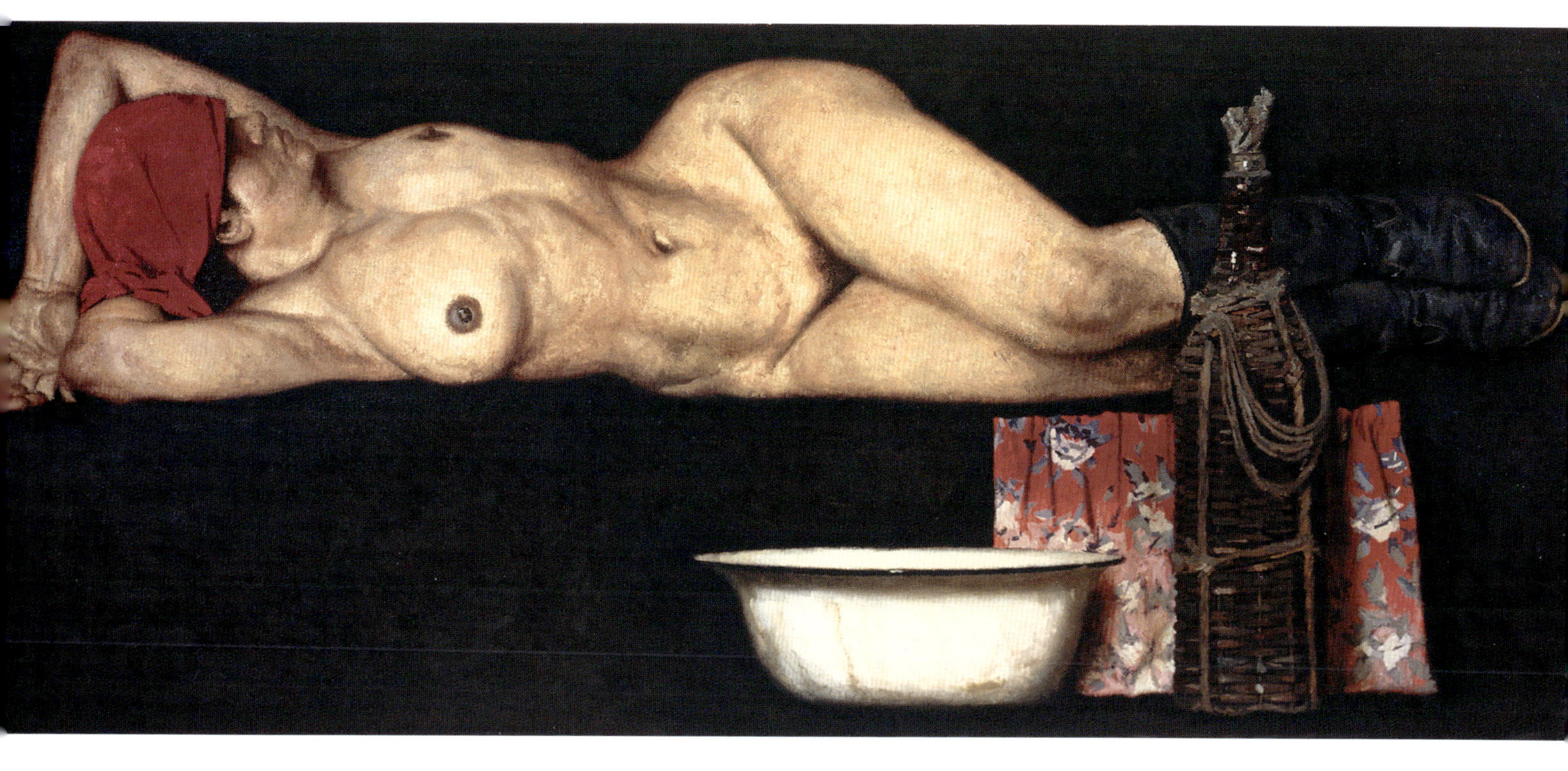

Mai V. DANTSIG

Born in 1930

Unmade Bed. 1986
78⅞ x 86¾ in.
(200,3 x 220,3 cm)
From a Private American Collection
Loan arranged by
The Museum of Russian Art
Minneapolis, Minnesota USA

With Tair Salakhov and Viktor Popkov, his fellow students at the Surikov Institute, Dantsig determined new tendencies in the Severe Style of the Russian art of the second half of the 20th century, rendering romantically in his paintings the harsh realities of life. The soft hues in his earlier undemanding landscapes gave way to more expressive and energetic colors in his later works. Although influenced by Deineka's art and Nissky's industrial landscapes, Dantsig's canvases declare his own comprehension of modern life.

Dantsig often uses large formats when painting. His expressive manner of depiction transforms the pictorial themes from routine to important, making his works appear monumental. His works become symbols or metaphors, characteristic of the Severe Style. Unmade Bed is a type of self portrait: The viewer can't see him on the canvas, but can get a sense of him through his personal belongings. Simple things present an image of a personality who is responsible for his own future, the future of his intimates as well as of his country. It was the theme of the strengthening of human dignity and independence that was developed by the Severe Style artists.

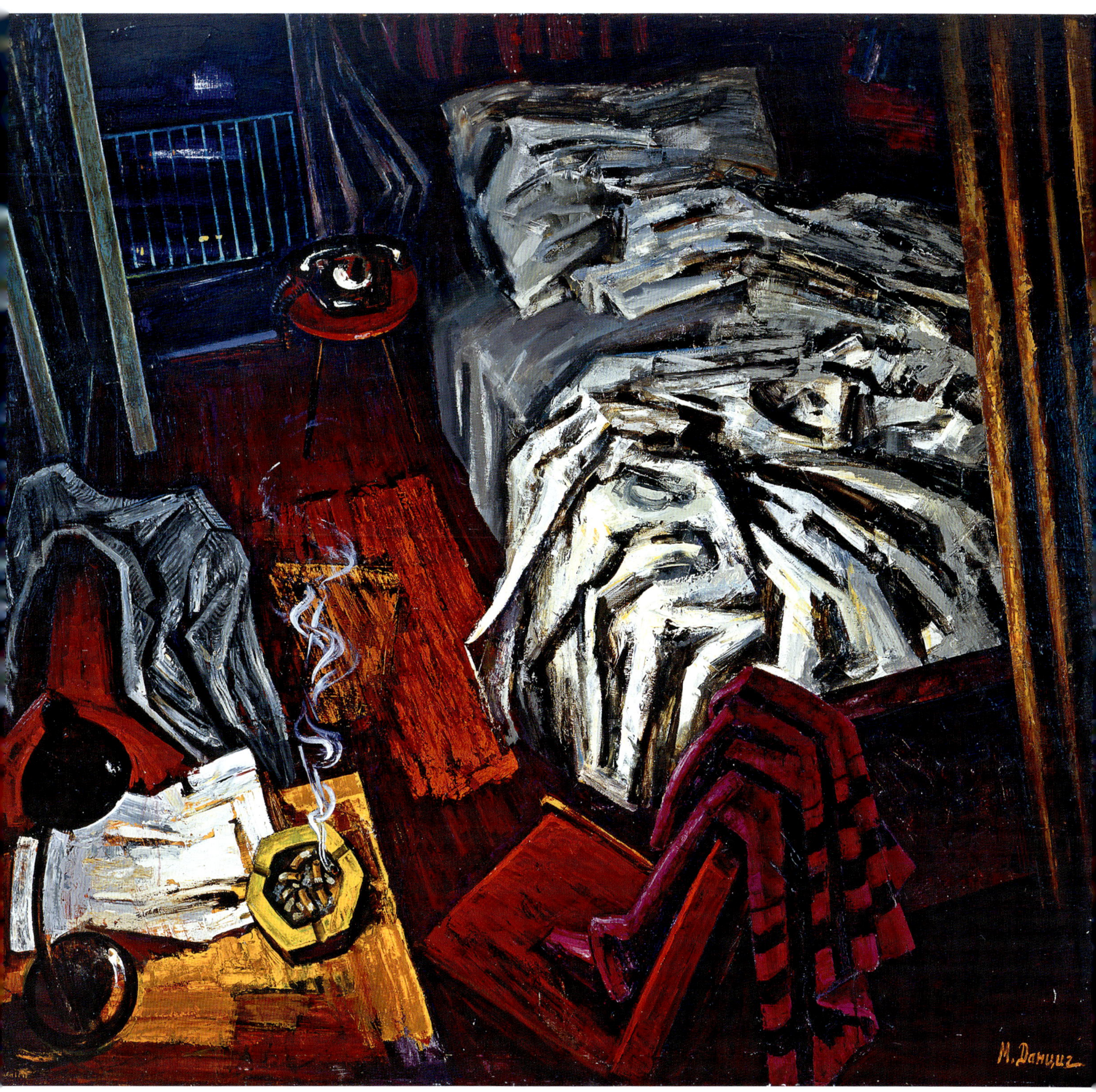
М. Данциг

Index